Home Office Research Study 191

Domestic Violence: Findings from a new British Crime Survey self-completion questionnaire

by
Catriona Mirrlees-Black

A Research, Development and Statistics Directorate Report

London: Home Office

Home Office Research Studies

The Home Office Research Studies are reports on research undertaken by or on behalf of the Home Office. They cover the range of subjects for which the Home Secretary has responsibility. Titles in the series are listed at the back of this report (copies are available from the address on the back cover). Other publications produced by the Research, Development and Statistics Directorate include Research Findings, the Research Bulletin, Statistical Bulletins and Statistical Papers.

The Research, Development and Statistics Directorate

The Research, Development and Statistics Directorate is an integral part of the Home Office, serving the Ministers and the department itself, its services, Parliament and the public through research, development and statistics. Information and knowledge from these sources informs policy development and the management of programmes; their dissemination improves wider public understanding of matters of Home Office concern.

First published 1999

Application for reproduction should be made to the Information and Publications Group, Room 201, Home Office, 50 Queen Anne's Gate, London SW1H 9AT.

©Crown copyright 1999   ISBN   1 84082 193 0
ISSN   0072 6435

Foreword

This report presents the findings of a new computerised self-completion component on domestic violence, included as part of the 1996 British Crime Survey. The questionnaire was designed to maximise victims' willingness to report domestic assaults and threats to the survey. It therefore provides the most reliable findings to date on the extent of domestic violence in England and Wales, and shows it to be prevalent.

Although the Home Office takes the lead on domestic violence matters, it is an important issue for a number of government departments. An inter-departmental group on domestic violence has been convened to develop policy in this area. A statistics subgroup are considering how more comprehensive and consistent information can be collected on domestic violence to improve understanding of the relevant issues, and to allow evaluation of preventive measures. This report is an important contribution to this process.

CHRISTOPHER NUTTALL
Director of Research, Development and Statistics

January 1999

Acknowledgements

The domestic violence self-completion component was designed in conjuction with researchers from Social and Community Planning Research (SCPR) who conducted the survey on behalf of the Home Office. Particular thanks go to Jon Hales, Nina Stratford, Patten Smith and Kerry Sproston.

Within the Home Office, Pat Mayhew, Sharon Grace and Jonathan King provided valuable comments on the draft report.

Finally, this work was completely dependent on the co-operation of the British Crime Survey respondents who gave up their time to take part in the survey. Many thanks to all respondents and especially to those who revealed very personal experiences in the domestic violence questionnaire.

CATRIONA MIRRLEES-BLACK

Contents

Summary

The 1996 British Crime Survey included a new computerised self-completion questionnaire designed to give the most reliable findings to date on the extent of domestic violence in England and Wales. The self-completion questionnaire increased respondents' willingness to report incidents by maximising anonymity and confidentiality. It also encouraged reporting of incidents victims did not define as 'crimes'. The questionnaire covered physical assaults and frightening threats committed by current and former partners against men and women aged 16 to 59.

Current levels of domestic violence

*   4.2% of women and 4.2% of men said they had been physically assaulted by a current or former partner in the last year. 4.9% of men and 5.9% of women had experienced physical assault and/or frightening threats. These levels are considerably higher than figures from other BCS measures.

*   Women were twice as likely as men to have been injured by a partner in the last year, and three times as likely to have suffered frightening threats. They were also more likely to have been assaulted three or more times.

*   In total it is estimated that there were about 6.6 million incidents of domestic physical assault in 1995. 2.9 million of these involved injury. In addition, there were about 7 million frightening threats.

Life-time experience

*   Women were far more likely to say they had experienced domestic assault at some time in their lives: 23% of women and 15% of men aged 16 to 59 said they had been physically assaulted by a current or

former partner at some time. The inclusion of frightening threats increases these figures to 26% and 17% respectively.

- At least 12% of women and 5% of men had been assaulted on three or more occasions. They were termed chronic victims.

- Young women aged 20 to 24 reported the highest levels of domestic violence to the survey: 28% said that they had been assaulted by a partner at some time, and 34% had been threatened or assaulted. Although the higher risk for young people tends to suggest domestic violence is increasing, it may also reflect a greater reluctance on the part of older victims to mention domestic assaults to the survey, or that incidents longer ago are less likely to be recalled in the survey context.

The victims

- Amongst women, risks of physical assault in 1995 were highest for those who were: aged 16 to 24; separated from their spouse; council tenants; in poor health; and/or, in financial difficulties.

- Amongst men, victimisation levels were highest for 16- to 24-year-olds; cohabiters; the unemployed; and again those in financial difficulties.

The assaults

- Pushing, shoving and grabbing are the most common type of assault. But kicking, slapping and hitting with fists took place in nearly half of incidents.

- The victim was injured in 41% of incidents. Women were more likely to be injured (47%) than men (31%). Although injury was usually restricted to bruising, 9% of incidents resulted in cuts and 2% in broken bones.

- Nearly all victims admitted they were upset by the experience, with women more likely to say so than men. The majority of female victims said they had been very frightened, compared to a minority of men.

- Of victims who had children in the household, about a third said the children had been aware of the last assault they had experienced.

- Chronic victims experienced more serious types of attack: they were more likely to be physically injured and were more emotionally affected by their experience. Three-quarters of the chronic victims were women.

The assailants

- Virtually all incidents against women reported to the survey were committed by men (99%). 95% of those against men were committed by women.

- The assailant was said to be under the influence of alcohol in 32% of incidents, and of drugs in 5%.

- Half of life-time incidents were committed by a current or former spouse compared to 43% of last-year incidents, probably reflecting lower rates of marriage amongst the younger age groups.

- The majority of life-time victims were living with their assailant at the time of the most recent assault: older victims more often so than younger ones.

- A half of those who were living with their assailant were still doing so at the time of the BCS interview. Women were less likely to still be living with their assailant than men, and chronic victims less likely than intermittent.

Victims' perceptions of their experiences

- Although the questions asked about incidents that would meet the legal definition of an assault, only 17% of incidents counted by the survey were considered to be crimes by their victims. Virtually no male victims defined their experience as a crime, while only four in ten chronic female victims did so.

- Victims were more likely to agree their experience made them "a victim of domestic violence" than a victim of a crime - overall, one-third did so. Women, and in particular chronic female victims, were much more likely to say so than men.

Support and advice

- About half of victims had told someone about their most recent assault: most often a friend, neighbour or relative.

- The police were told of 12% of incidents overall, and 22% of those against female chronic victims. They offered advice or support in 60% of incidents, which was found helpful in 40% of cases they were told about.

- Medical staff were the next most likely to hear of incidents (they were told about 10% of all incidents), and were more likely to offer advice and support than the police (they did so in 70% of incidents they were told about).

- Victims who had been injured, frightened or upset, or whose children were aware of the incident were the most likely to tell someone about their experience.

- Victims' perceptions of their experiences influence willingness to take up available services. Respondents who believed they had experienced a crime or were victims of domestic violence were far more likely to have told others about it. For instance, incidents preceived as 'crimes' were more likely to be reported to the police: 34% were, compared to an overall reporting rate of 12%. Also, victims who felt to blame in some way were the less likely to report incidents to the police.

I Introduction

This paper presents the findings of a new computer-assisted self-interviewing (CASI) questionnaire on domestic violence, used in the 1996 British Crime Survey (BCS). The confidential nature of this method of interviewing, together with the large and representative sample size of the BCS mean that these findings are likely to be the most reliable to date on the extent of domestic violence in England and Wales.

Defining domestic violence

The term 'domestic violence' can encompass a wide range of experiences. The measures used in research vary considerably as to the type of relationship they count as 'domestic' and the types of experience that are deemed 'violence'.

What is 'domestic'?

Clearly, the wider the definition of domestic relationships, the higher are the estimates of domestic violence. The narrowest definition restricts domestic violence to that between people currently living together as couples, and often only as heterosexual couples. Estimates can vary on whether they classify incidents as 'domestic' that occur between people in the early stages of a relationship who do not know each other well, and those where there is no longer an intimate relationship but there has been at sometime in the past. The definition used in the CASI questionnaire encompasses all intimate relationships, whether or not there is, or has been, co-habitation. The police, however, tend to take somewhat broader criteria, describing incidents as 'domestic' that involve people who are related in any way or who live in the same household. This might include assaults on children by parents and vice versa.

What is 'violence'?

Deciding what constitutes violence is not straightforward either. One option is to include all forms of physical assault and attempted assault, however minor and for whatever reason they were committed. Some commentators, though, suggest violent acts are only those where there is an intent to cause some harm, in particular pain or injury (Gelles, 1997).[1] By only questioning victims, though, it is not possible to know for sure the intention of the assailant.

The victim's judgement of whether the force used is acceptable may also be relevant. However, it would be dangerous to assume that just because the recipient judges the behaviour as normal and acceptable, society would generally agree.

Physical violence is not the only way to inflict harm against a partner. A wider definition of violence would include bullying, psychologically controlling and emotionally abusive behaviour. The effects of these can be as great, if not greater (Straus and Sweet, 1992). They are also considerably more difficult to measure.

Measuring domestic violence

There is thus much debate on the 'best' way to measure domestic victimisation (eg Nazroo, 1995, Römkens, 1997, Smith, 1994, Stanko, 1988). In truth, there is unlikely to be one best way. Undoubtedly different methods give different findings, but these should be viewed as complementary rather than competitive. Although probing qualitative interviews will give a better picture of the nature and context of victimisation, they can only realistically be done on a small scale and are not, therefore, appropriate for estimating the extent of victimisation at a national level. Structured quantitative type methods, on the other hand, can be carried out on a larger scale so that findings can be generalised if samples are representative of the population they are intended to describe. If repeated in the same way, they are useful for drawing comparisons across time and populations. The inflexibility of the quantitative method does, however, mean that the nuances of individual experiences are unlikely to be adequately described.[2]

British Crime Survey measures

The purpose of the British Crime Survey (BCS) is to give estimates of the extent of household and personal crime in England and Wales, to track trends in these, and to describe the relative risks for different population groups. There are many constraints on a large-scale survey such as this, an

---

1 Gelles (1997) differentiates between 'normal violence' and 'abusive violence', the former being 'commonplace slaps, pushes, shoves, and spankings that frequently are considered a normal or acceptable part ... of interacting with a spouse'. Violence becomes abusive, he suggests, when there is a high potential for injuring the recipient.

2 An alternative approach is to survey men's attitudes towards committing domestic violence and admitted abusive behaviour (Leibrich, Paulin and Ransom, 1995)

important one being interview length. The BCS necessarily, therefore, takes a very structured approach to measurement.

The BCS has been measuring the extent of crime against adults living in private households since 1982. Face-to-face interviews are conducted with a large number of adults who are representative of the household population of England and Wales. The 1996 survey, which this report refers to, interviewed over 16,000 people (Mirrlees-Black et al, 1996). For the types of crime it covers, it provides the best estimates of their extent and trends over time. This is because the majority of crimes are not reported to the police and those that are are not necessarily recorded by them. Police figures also give very little information about the victims of crime, the offenders, or any detail about what occurred.[3] The police do separately record domestic *incidents* reported to command and control units, although what they include in this category seems to vary considerably by force (Yarwood 1997).

Until now, the BCS has measured domestic violence in two ways. First, the main crime counting component gives estimates of the incidence of domestic violence against men and women in the calendar year preceding the survey. This measure is available for all sweeps of the BCS: the 1996 estimates were published with the main BCS findings (Mirrlees-Black et al, 1996). Second, the 1992 BCS measured women's *lifetime* experience of domestic violence in a separate set of questions (Mirrlees-Black,1995). Women who had lived with a partner at some time were asked which five options best applied to their relationships, ranging from 'there have never been any arguments' to 'treatment for physical violence from a doctor or nurse has frequently been required'. The findings are discussed in Chapter 2.

The BCS measures have concentrated on physical assault for a number of reasons. Firstly, as noted above, measuring other forms of abuse is not straightforward. Secondly, the BCS is primarily a measure of 'crime', and psychological abuse usually does not meet the legal criteria of a crime.[4] To match as closely as possible the police count of domestic incidents, the main crime counting component (called the 'victim form measure' hereafter) has tended to define domestic violence as woundings and common assaults committed by any household member or relative.[5]

---

[3] Some police forces collect this type of information, but it is not routinely available at a national level. Ad hoc surveys of forces have been conducted to gather this type of information centrally, eg Davidoff & Dowds (1989) and Watson (1996).

[4] This has changed recently with the introduction of the Protection from Harassment Act 1997 which made certain types of harassment a crime. Also, Part IV of the Family Law Act 1996 introduced non-molestation and non-occupation orders which can be used to prevent psychological abuse.

[5] The victim form measure can be recalculated to cover only partner and ex-partner violence, and to include serious threats.

Other UK measures of domestic violence

Although there are no other large-scale national surveys of the extent of domestic violence in England and Wales, there have been some small-scale surveys, mainly in particular localities, and/or of particular groups. The findings of five such surveys are summarised in Appendix B. Nationally representative samples, such as the BCS, provide national level estimates of risk but may not have adequate samples to reliably assess differential risks for particular areas or groups of people. Local surveys and surveys of particular groups fill this gap, but unfortunately are not always conducted on sound methodologial grounds, or do not give sufficient details of method to assess their reliability (Mirrlees-Black,1995).

National surveys

There have been a number of other national surveys, using a variety of methodologies. The 1996 Scottish Crime Survey included a paper self-completion questionnaire based on the BCS version. Findings are due to be published in late 1998. The USA's National Crime Victimisation Survey adopts a similar methodology to the main BCS crime counting component. This has recently been modified to improve the measurement of violence within families (Bachman and Taylor, 1994). Canada (Statistics Canada, 1993), the Netherlands (Römkens, 1997), New Zealand (New Zealand Ministry of Justice, 1996) and Australia (Australian Bureau of Statistics, 1996), on the other hand, have chosen to conduct surveys designed specially to measure only violence against women. The details of these surveys are discussed in Appendix C.

The new CASI questionnaire in the 1996 BCS

Although social surveys will give more reliable estimates of the true extent of domestic violence than administrative data such as that recorded by the police or other agencies dealing with victims, a survey approach is not without problems. In addition to the usual errors associated with sample surveys (see Appendix D), there are additional problems specific to domestic violence. Such incidents tend to be of a personal nature and victims may be reluctant to reveal them to interviewers. Surveys conducted in respondents' homes must also take account of the presence of other household members during interviews, especially where this may have implications for the safety of respondents. A further problem is that victims may not define their experiences as falling within the remit of a 'crime' survey.

To improve measurement, the 1996 BCS included a specially designed computer-assisted self-interviewing (CASI) component for both men and women aged 16-59. The self-completion format emphasised anonymity and confidentiality, and the questions were designed to cover a wide range of experiences. The CASI questionnaire appears to have been successful in these respects and may be repeated on an ad hoc basis in future surveys.[6]

In the CASI questionnaire, domestic violence was defined to include only incidents between people who were currently, or had been, in an 'intimate' relationship. Same sex relationships were counted. Although only incidents between 'intimates' were measured, the intention was to distinguish those between people living together, people who were married, and people no longer in relationships.[7]

Although the CASI questionnaire concentrates on physical assault, estimates of the use of serious threats can also be derived to give at least an indication of levels of more psychological abuse. Limitations on the length of CASI questionnaires precluded collecting details of serious threats.

Structure of the report

The next chapter reviews the three BCS measures of domestic violence, and compares the estimates of the extent of domestic violence derived from each. Chapter 3 looks in more detail at the CASI estimates of the prevalence and incidence of domestic victimisation (both physical assaults and serious threats). Chapter 4 describes who is most at risk of experiencing domestic assault, while Chapter 5 looks at the type of violence used and the physical and emotional consequences to victims. Chapter 6 gives some information on the assailants in domestic incidents. Chapter 7 looks at the support and advice that victims seek, and how useful they have found it. Chapter 8 asks whether victims define themselves as victims of crime and/or of domestic violence. Finally, Chapter 9 highlights the key policy relevant findings.

---

6   There is a maximum length of the BCS questionnaire in terms of what respondents can cope with. There is, therefore, a limit to the number of CASI topics that can be included in each survey. The first BCS to use CASI, in 1994, covered sexual victimisation. In the 1998 BCS there was a CASI component on harassment/stalking.

7   In the event, due to a routing error in the CASI programme, it was not possible to distinguish between current and former relationships.

2 Comparing BCS measures

This chapter compares the methods and key findings from the three British Crime Survey measures of domestic victimisation: the calendar year rates derived from the main crime counting component included in all sweeps of the survey; the 1992 measure of life-time experience; and the 1996 computerised self-completion component.

Main crime count - all BCS sweeps

The main purpose of the BCS is to provide a count of crime that is unaffected by variations in people's propensity to report crimes to the police and in police recording practice. It does this by collecting detailed information about incidents respondents have experienced and coding these according to legal definitions of offences. All sweeps of the BCS since 1982 have gathered details of violent offences, within which domestic incidents can be separately identified. Each sweep measures the number of incidents in the previous year. The 1996 survey, therefore, gives a count of domestic violence in 1995.

Eliciting incidents from respondents is a two-stage process. Firstly, they are asked up to 25 'screener' questions which are couched in everyday language. Domestic violence incidents may be mentioned at any of these screeners but tend to come from the general assault screener (53%), the threat screener (19%) and the domestic assault screener (27%). The first two are read out loud by the interviewer. The domestic assault screener is presented on a card with the following wording:

> Apart from anything you have already mentioned, since the first of January 1995 has any member of your household (aged 16 or over) deliberately hit you with their fists or with a weapon of any sort or kicked you, or used force or violence on you in any other way?

Up to six discrete incidents are followed up in a detailed 'victim form'. This gathers information on what exactly happened, and when and where. It also records details of the offender and the consequence of the incident for the victim. 'Series' incidents - similar incidents probably committed by the same person - are followed up by just one victim form, and that victim form is taken as representative of all the incidents in the series. All questions on the victim form are asked out loud by the interviewer. Interviewers have the option of skipping victim forms relating to incidents picked up by the domestic violence screener if others are present, and they can call back at a more suitable time to complete these.

By calculating the number of incidents of a particular type experienced by BCS respondents within the last calendar year, and multiplying this up by the current population of adults in England and Wales, it is possible to derive estimates of the total number of crimes committed.

It is also possible to derive estimates of particular types of crime, according to, for instance, where it occurred or who committed it. The main 1996 BCS report used a typology of all violent crime in which the offender had some physical contact with the victim. (The offences covered were wounding, common assault, robbery and snatch theft.[1]) The typology distinguishes violent incidents according to the relationship between offender(s) and victim, producing three categories: acquaintance violence; stranger violence; and domestic violence. A fourth category in the typology was 'mugging', covering robbery and snatch theft.

Domestic violence was defined as those incidents involving partners, ex-partners, household members and other relatives, regardless of where they took place. A respondent was counted as a victim of domestic violence if they had suffered one or more such incidents in the previous year. This definition was designed to match most closely ad hoc police measures of domestic violence (Davidoff and Dowds, 1989).

Incidence

The 1996 BCS estimated that in 1995 there were one million incidents of domestic violence, of which two-thirds were against women and one-third against men (Mirrlees-Black et al, 1996). Domestic violence accounted for a quarter (24%) of all violent incidents measured by the BCS that year.

There has been an upward trend in the number of domestic violence incidents recorded by the survey (Table A.2.1). Between 1981 and 1995 the number of all violent incidents increased by 88%, but domestic violence increased by 242%. As the survey measured much larger increases in violence among people who knew each other than between strangers, it is

---

1   Sexual violence, although included in the survey, is omitted: findings are unreliable due to the small number of incidents about which details were given to interviewers.

Figure 2.1 Trends in prevalence rates for domestic violence 1981 to 1995

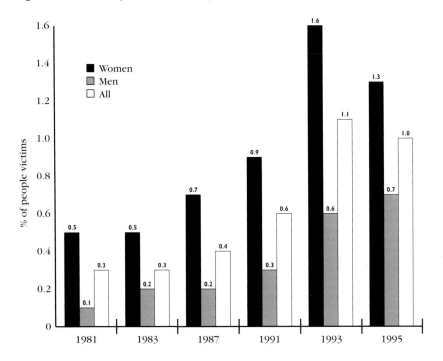

plausible that at least part of this increase is due to victims being more willing to tell survey interviewers about such experiences.

Prevalence

One per cent of all BCS respondents (that is people aged 16 or older) had experienced one or more incidents of domestic violence in 1995. The proportions were 0.7% of men, and 1.3% of women. Half of victims had only experienced one such incident in the year, a fifth two, and the remaining third, three or more.

Figure 2.1 (and Table A.2.2) shows trends in the proportion of respondents reporting domestic violence to the survey since the first sweep in 1982. The 1994 sweep of the survey saw the inclusion of the domestic violence screener questions for the first time.[2] As this screener picked up additional incidents to those reported on the general assault screeners, some of the increase between 1991 and 1993 is due to this methodological change. However, the number of incidents against women fell back again in 1995.

---

2   The screener was first included in the 1992 survey on a pilot basis, but incidents elicited by the screener were not followed up by victim forms.

The victim form rates can be recalculated to cover a different definition of 'domestic' and of 'violence'. Counting only those incidents committed by current or former partners gives an overall prevalence rate of 0.6% for 1995: 1.0% of women and 0.3% of men.[3] Expanding the definition of domestic violence to include serious threats, such as threats to kill or harm, gives prevalence rates of 1.7% for women and 0.5% for men.

1992 Life-time measure

Incident-based measures of domestic violence such as those derived from the BCS victim form count, have been criticised for failing to take account of the serial and ongoing nature of domestic violence. The 1992 BCS included a measure designed to take account of this (Mirrlees-Black, 1995).

Women who had lived with a partner at some time were asked a question intended to measure their life-time experience of domestic violence. Respondents were told that the aim was to 'measure the real level of domestic violence in Britain'. They were handed a card with the following question: 'Thinking about both past and present relationships, which of the following statements applies?', and were asked to give the number corresponding to their chosen option (listed in Table 2.1).

The question deliberately focused on only a sub-set of relationships (the word 'relationships' was used to avoid any mention of a specific party). It explicitly excluded psychological violence and may be taken to exclude sexual violence. There are some possible problems with the question. There is no definition of what physical violence is, so the term may have been interpreted in different ways by different people. Also, it required that, at the top end of the scale, medical treatment was sought whereas it might deliberately have been avoided. Reading and responding to the question, furthermore, required a reasonable level of literacy, a problem with most current self-completion methodologies.

Overall, 11% of women who had lived with a partner at some time said there had been a degree of physical violence in their relationship(s). Most had not received medical attention (Table 2.1). Paradoxically, although older women have had more time in which to experience violence from a partner, it was younger women who were more likely to say they had done so. Possible explanations include:

---

3   For 16- to 59-year-olds, the prevalence of partner violence on the 1996 victim form measure was 1.3% for women and 0.4% for men.

- As younger women tend to have younger partners, it may be that younger men now are more likely to act violently than younger men in the past.

- Younger women now tend to live with a greater number of partners, so increasing their chances of encountering one that is violent.

- Older women may be more reticent to tell others about their experiences, or to define their experiences as relevant to the survey.

- If incidents are more likely to occur when women are young, older women's experiences will have been longer ago. Older women may be less likely to recall longer ago incidents in the survey context, or have favourably revised their memories over time.

Table 2.1 Women's lifetime experience of domestic violence during past and present relationships (1992 BCS)

	18 to 29	30 to 59	60 and over	All
	%	%	%	%
There have never been any arguments	12	15	24	17
There have been arguments from time to time, but never any physical violence	71	73	73	73
There has been some physical violence but nothing that has ever needed treatment from a doctor or nurse	14	9	2	8
There has been some physical violence and treatment from a doctor or nurse has occasionally been required	2	3	1	2
There has been physical violence and treatment from a doctor or nurse has frequently been required	1	1	<1	1
Unweighted N	379	1163	799	2341

Notes:
1.   Source: 1992 BCS, core sample.
2.   Base = women aged 18 and over who have lived with a partner at some time.

The 1996 Computer-Assisted Self-Interviewing (CASI) measure

The switch from paper and pen to Computer-Assisted Personal Interviewing (CAPI) in the 1994 BCS gave the opportunity to introduce Computer-Assisted Self-Interviewing (CASI). Following the main interview, which is conducted by an interviewer in the usual way, the laptop computer is passed to the respondent, who reads the questions on the screen and inputs their responses directly into the computer. A comparison of paper self-completion and CASI methods for measuring illegal drug use in the 1992 and 1994 BCSs respectively, found not only improved data quality (because respondents cannot skip questions) but suggested respondents perceived increased confidentiality for their responses (Mayhew, 1995). The method was also used in the 1994 BCS to estimate the extent of sexual victimisation against women (Percy and Mayhew, 1997). This gave a much higher count of incidents (over ten times higher) than that from the main crime counting component of the BCS.[4]

In the 1996 BCS the drug misuse questions were again included, providing a relatively straightforward warm-up for the more complex domestic violence questionnaire. As in 1994, respondents aged 60 or over were not required to tackle the self-completion. This is mainly because there is a gradual fall in the proportion of respondents willing to undertake CASI with age (see Appendix D).

An important element of the design was the description of relationships to be covered by the questions. In order to match as many definitions of domestic violence as possible it had to include current and former 'intimate' relationships, however enduring, and same-sex relationships.[5] The questionnaire was extensively piloted on men and women but of particular importance were the tests by groups of women at Women's Refuges. The main changes following this test were an additional question on whether children were present during the incident, and expansion of the questions on contact with various agencies to include an assessment of the level of service received.

There was a two-stage structure to the questionnaire. The first set of questions explored whether the respondent had ever been:

- sworn at or insulted by a current or former partner;

---

4   But, as discussed by the authors, it was not possible to identify what, if any, criminal offences victims had experienced. This was partly because of problems designing questions to measure sexual offences, and partly due to limitations on the amount of detail about experiences that could be collected from victims using the CASI methodology.

5   CASI programming provided some assistance in that the questions referring to current and former spouses were only asked of respondents who had ever been married.

- had things said to them that frightened them, such as threats to harm their children;

- had any physical force used against them by a current or former partner, such as grabbing, pushing, shaking or hitting;

- and, for those who had had force used against them in the previous year, whether they had been injured, even slightly, on any of these occasions.

The second set of questions asked the respondent to describe the nature and circumstances of the most recent incident they had experienced, however long ago this was.

As noted above, the two main problems of using crime surveys to measure domestic violence are firstly, the understandable reluctance of respondents to divulge such experiences to survey interviewers, and secondly, a reluctance on the part of victims to define their experience as falling within the remit of a crime survey. Each of these points was addressed by the design of the 1996 BCS self-completion questionnaire.

Anonymity and confidentiality

The self-completion format allows respondents a greater sense of anonymity: telling a non-judgemental computer may be easier than telling a person. There should also be a greater degree of confidentiality. This is particularly important for domestic violence, where the other party involved may well be present. Researchers also have an ethical responsibility to ensure respondents are not harmed by having participated in research. To address this, interviewers who felt it unwise to proceed with the domestic violence component could abort this stage of the interview. They had the option of arranging a later appointment to complete these questions. Also, once the respondent had completed the section their answers were electronically hidden so that no access to the responses was possible until the data were downloaded centrally by the research company.

One indication that this method succeeded in convincing respondents of the confidentiality of the process was the proportion of incidents reported to the survey that had not been told to anyone else.[6] This was about half of most recent incidents (see Chapter 8 for further details).

---

6   Though, or course, there may be reasons for not having told anyone else, other than it was considered too personal or confidential.

Including non-criminal incidents

The questions were designed to broaden the context of the survey beyond crime. Thus, the first question concerned behaviours that were clearly non-criminal: having been sworn at or insulted by a partner.[7] We know from subsequent qualitative work, however, that some respondents found this question difficult to answer in the crime context of the survey (White and Lewis, 1998). They wanted to refer to serious experiences. The question was designed to elicit a 'yes' response from the majority of respondents, the idea being that having said 'yes' to one question would make it easier to say 'yes' to subsequent questions. In fact, only about half of both men and women said they had been sworn at or insulted at some time in a relationship.

Nonetheless, there is evidence that incidents not defined by respondents as 'crimes' were mentioned. This comes from answers to a question that asked whether the respondent felt the last incident they had experienced was: a crime, wrong but not a crime, or just something that happens. Just 17% of incidents were said to be crimes. A further third were considered to be 'wrong', but the largest category - 45% of incidents - were 'just something that happens' (Table A.2.3). Women were more likely to judge incidents as crimes, as were victims of more than one or two such incidents. There is further discussion of these findings in Chapter 7.

Comparison of BCS estimates

Table 2.2 compares estimates from the three BCS measures of the prevalence of domestic violence - that is the proportion of people victimised once or more. The age range has been restricted to 16- to 59-year-olds so that comparisons can be made with the CASI measure.

According to the 1992 domestic violence question, 13.6% of 16- to 59-year-old women who had lived with a partner had suffered physical violence in a relationship at some time in their lives, and 3.6% said this had resulted in injury. This compares with 22.7% of women and 14.9% of men who reported some type of physical assault in the 1996 CASI. This difference is not really surprising. The 1992 BCS question was far more explicit in stating that it was intended to measure domestic violence and perhaps, by implication, suggested that 'one off' incidents were not being asked about.

The victim form based measure only covers incidents occurring within the calendar year previous to the survey. It gives significantly lower estimates of last-year prevalence than the CASI self-report questionnaire: in this, 4.2% of

---

7 BCS respondents are also asked about other matters clearly not concerned with criminal victimisation experience: eg experience of household fires, and everyday contacts with the police. Respondents had also previously completed questions on knowledge and use of illegal drugs.

men and women said they had been assaulted in some way by a partner, compared with 1.3% of women and 0.4% of men according to the victim forms.[8] The gap is even wider when serious threats are included in the counts.

The advantage of the victim form count, though, is that as a by-product of the main crime counting component of the BCS, it is available for all sweeps of the survey. The victim form measure also has the advantage of a high degree of confidence that incidents included meet the legal definition of a crime. The CASI method limits the amount of detail that can be collected about incidents: all questions are pre-coded so that respondents only have to type one key in response. This means no 'open-ended' information about the context or nature of incidents is gathered, so there is no real check on what exactly is being counted.

Table 2.2 Prevalence of domestic victimisation: comparison of BCS estimates

		Women 16-59		Men 16-59	
	1992 BCS	1996 BCS (Victim forms)[3]	1996 BCS (CASI)	1996 BCS (Victim forms)[3]	1996 BCS (CASI)
	%	%	%	%	%
Life-time assault	13.6	na	22.7	na	14.9
Life-time injury assault	3.6	na	na	na	na
Last-year assault	na	1.3	4.2	0.4	4.2
Last-year injury assault	na	1.0	2.2	0.2	1.1
Last-year assault or threat	na	1.7	5.9	0.5	4.9

Note:
1. Source: 1992 and 1996 British Crime Survey core samples.
2. Base for estimates are: 1992 - women aged 16 to 59 who had lived with a partner at some time (83% of all) (sample = 1560). 1996 victim form - all 16- to 59-year-olds (sample= 6098 women and 5146 men). 1996 CASI - men/women aged 16 to 59 who have ever been married, had a partner, or a boy/girl-friend and who accepted the questionnaire (97% of all).
3. The victim form measure is of violence committed by a current or former partner against 16- to 59-year-olds only. This is narrower than the definition in Mirrlees-Black et al (1996) which covered all adults aged 16 and over and additionally included violence committed by other household members and all relatives.

The variations in the estimates demonstrate the effects of different approaches to measurement. Some aspects of these - such as increasing confidentiality and anonymity - will tend to increase the validity of estimates. Other differences are essentially definitional, and reflect survey assumptions about the types of experience that fall within the scope of domestic violence.

Chapter 3 covers the findings of the CASI method on the extent of victimisation in further detail.

---

8 Although more respondents admitted to recent assault on the CASI questionnaire than the victim form measure, not all those who had reported incidents that were subsequently coded as domestic violence on a victim form mentioned an assault on CASI (Table A.2.4). In some cases this is because the incident occurred between 1 January 1995 and the beginning of the 12 month time frame of the CASI questionnaire.

3 Extent of domestic violence

This chapter reports the CASI estimates of the proportion of 16- to 59-year-olds in England and Wales who have experienced domestic victimisation (physical assault and serious threats) and the number of such incidents that occurred in 1995.

Crime surveys have been criticised for concentrating on annual (or 'last-year') victimisation rates. This is particularly so with regard to more ongoing forms of victimisation such as domestic violence, which may not easily be located into limited time frames and into discrete and definitionally tidy events (Genn, 1988). Nonetheless, there is inescapable demand for estimates of the current extent of victimisation, and a 'last-year' measure has a role here. Moreover, people's ability to remember events accurately is poorer with longer time frames. As serious incidents are more memorable, longer time frames will produce a bias towards more serious incidents.

A life-time prevalence measure has value too. It captures repeat victimisation better than a one-year time frame, and gives a count of the total number of people affected by domestic violence. It is also more appropriate for differentiating between victims and non-victims (given that a one-year time frame omits other than recent victims), and for assessing the long-term consequences of victimisation. Another benefit is that the recently victimised, for reasons of their own safety, may move to non-household accommodation such as refuges, and thus not be included in a household survey. This will tend to affect 'last-year' estimates more than 'life-time' ones.

The CASI questionnaire, therefore, asked about both life-time and last-year experiences. Physical violence was measured by a question asking about the use of force (for which grabbing, pushing, shaking and hitting were given as examples). Non-physical violence was measured by asking respondents whether a partner had ever said frightening things to them, such as threatening to harm them, or someone close to them. Children were given as an example of the latter if there were currently children living in the household. Physical violence by a partner is called 'domestic assault' here, and things said to frighten the victim are called 'frightening threats'.

Life-time experience

Among 16- to 59-year-olds, 23% of women, and 15% of men said they had experienced an assault from a current or former partner at some time in their lives (Figure 3.1 and Table A.3.1).[1] Combining frightening threats and assaults gives an overall estimate that 26% of women and 17% of men have suffered from physical or non-physical violence from a partner at some time.

Figure 3.1 Life-time prevalence of domestic violence

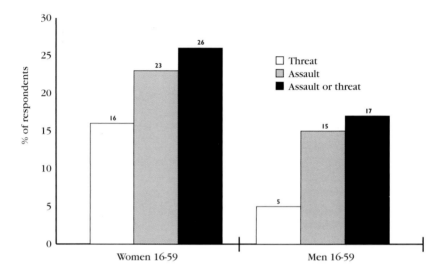

Of the BCS sample that were, or had been married, 18% of women and 13% of men said they had been assaulted by a current or ex-spouse at some time. For frightening threats, the figures were 13% and 5% respectively.

Although the 'opportunity' to have experienced domestic violence increases with age, life-time prevalence levels do not show a consistent increase with age. Figures 3.2 and 3.3 show the proportion within each age group experiencing domestic assault only, frightening threats only, or both in their lifetime, for women and men respectively. (Table A.3.2 shows prevalence estimates for each separately.)

Amongst women, it was the 20- to 24-year-olds who were most likely to say they had experienced some type of domestic violence in their lifetime. A third had experienced any type of violence; 28% one involving assault; and

---

1   The base excludes 50 men and 15 women who said they had never had a partner. Their exclusion does not affect the estimates.

Figure 3.2 Life-time prevalence for women

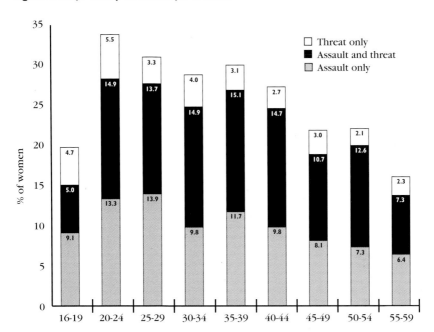

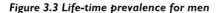

Figure 3.3 Life-time prevalence for men

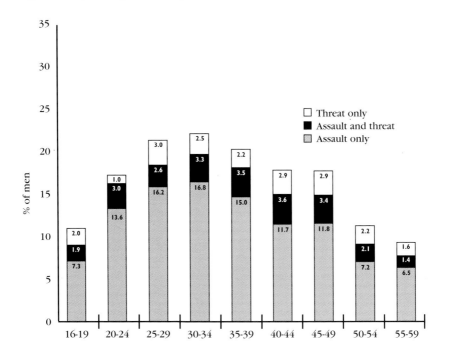

20% one involving frightening threats. Women were far more likely than men to have experienced both assault and threats (the darkest bar on the charts).

Amongst men, it was the 30-34-year-olds who were most likely to have been victims: 23% had experienced assault, threats or both; 20% assault; and 6% threats.

For men and women, the oldest age group were the least likely to report such experiences to the BCS. This may seem to suggest that risks of domestic violence have increased over time. Chapter 4 shows violence is most common for young people, by looking at the age of victims of recent incidents (see also Table A.3.3). Any increase is, therefore, likely to be seen in increased risks for young people. It may be that the younger generation now tend to have a greater number of 'domestic' relationships, and hence have increased their chances of encountering a 'violent' partner. Or, given young people tend to have young partners, it could be that younger people are now more violent towards their partners than in the past.

However, it is also plausible that risks of domestic violence have not changed and that the survey is undercounting incidents against older people. This may reflect a greater reluctance on the part of the older age groups to divulge their experiences to the survey.[2] Younger people may be more aware of domestic violence as a public issue and less inhibited about revealing such experiences. Also, given older people's experiences are more likely to have occurred sometime ago, they may be less likely to recall incidents in the survey context, or to have favourably revised their memories over time.

Last-year experience

Within the twelve months previous to the survey, 4.2% of both women and men aged 16 to 59 said they had been assaulted by a current or former partner (Figure 3.4, Table A.3.3). Last year victims of assault were asked whether they had been injured, even slightly, on any occasion within the year. Women were twice as likely to say they had: 2.2% said they had suffered injury at the hands of a partner compared to 1.1% of men. As with the life-time estimates, women were far more likely to say they had been on the receiving end of frightening threats: 3.8% said they had, compared to 1.2% of men. These findings suggest that the experiences of female victims are qualitatively different from that of most male victims. Not only are they more likely to be injured in assaults, they are also far more likely to be living in fear of their partners.

---

2   There is some evidence that older victims were less willing to report incidents to the survey. The incidents the older group mentioned were more likely to have already been reported to other people (police/medical profession).

Figure 3.4 Prevalence of domestic violence in last year

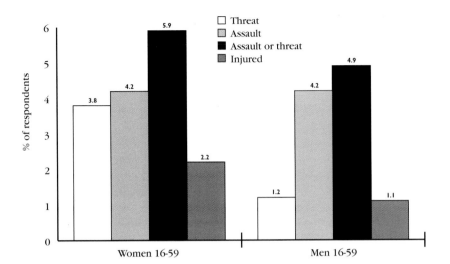

Frequency of victimisation

Victims who said they had been assaulted in the previous year were asked how often this had happened within the year.[3] The lowest level of frequency measured was 'once or twice', which may or may not have been interpreted as just one or two incidents.[4] It has been suggested that domestic violence is very rarely a one-off event. Certainly the level of repeat victimisation within the year was high, with about half of female victims of domestic assault and a third of male victims saying they had been assaulted three or more times (Figure 3.5 and Tables A.3.4 and A.3.5). Frightening threats were slightly more likely than assaults to be repeated within the year: about half of both male and female victims said it had happened three or more times.

Those who had been victims in the last year were asked to give an exact count of the number of times they had been assaulted and injured in the year. The average number of incidents of physical assault per female victim was 5.2, and per male victim it was 5.0. Looking just at those incidents resulting in injury, the average per female victim was 2.9, and per male victim was 1.5.

---

3   Victims of assault who had not experienced an assault within the last 12 months were separately asked how many times they had been assaulted in total.

4   This cannot be tested as a separate question asking for the exact number was not asked of those who gave the 'once or twice' response. In calculating the mean number of incidents, this response has been coded as an average of 1.5.

Figure 3.5 Number of incidents of domestic violence in last year

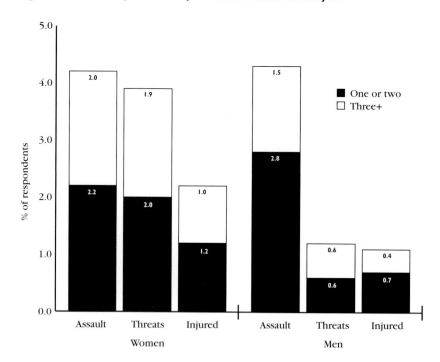

Number of incidents

The average number of incidents per victim can be used to give an estimate of the number of incidents of domestic violence occurring in the year in England and Wales. Because the BCS is based on a sample of respondents, the estimates are subject to sampling error. Table 3.1 gives the 'best' estimate of the number of incidents, together with the range within which the true value is very likely to be. It is estimated there were about 3.29 million incidents of domestic assault against women in 1995, 1.86 million of which resulted in injury. Additionally, women are estimated to have experienced over five million frightening threats. There were a similar number of domestic assaults against men (3.25 million), but a smaller proportion resulted in injury (1 million).[5] Men experienced far fewer frightening threats than women (1.98 million).

---

5   Although, on average, female victims are more likely to experience repeated assault, because there are more men aged 16 to 59 in the population than women, the total number of assaults is evenly split.

A typology of domestic assault

Due to limitations on the length of a CASI questionnaire, only details of incidents of physical violence (called 'domestic assault' here) were collected. The remainder of the report refers only to these, unless otherwise stated.

Table 3.1 Number of incidents of domestic violence in 1995

	Best estimate (millions)	Lowest estimate (millions)	Highest estimate (millions)
Women			
Domestic assault	3.29	2.62	3.97
- of which, injury assaults	1.86	1.28	2.44
Frightening threats	5.06	4.23	5.89
Men			
Domestic assault	3.25	2.47	4.04
- of which, injury assaults	1.00	0.42	1.57
Frightening threats	1.98	1.23	2.72

Note:
1. Source: 1996 BCS CASI questionnaire.
2. The number is calculated by multiplying the average number of incidents per victim by the number of men/women aged 16 to 59 in the population of England and Wales (women aged 16 to 59 = 15,058,000; men aged 16 to 59 = 15,415,000). The total number of incidents per victim were capped at 50 to avoid distorting effects of very high values. The ranges of estimates are based on 95% confidence intervals and assume a design effect of 1.2.

It is useful from a policy point of view to identify separately victims of repeated violence from those subject to more intermittent incidents. Repeat chronic victimisation suggests an abusive relationship in which violence is relatively likely to reoccur. The risks and nature of victimisation are, therefore, considered separately for victims who said they had been assaulted 'once or twice' ('intermittent' victims) and for those who reported three or more assaults to the survey ('chronic' victims). In reality, of course, levels of victimisation form a continuum, and the division into two categories is fairly artificial. For instance, women who had only recently entered a violent relationship may go on to become chronic victims. There is also an important limitation of this typology: it takes no account of the seriousness of the assaults to the victim (in physical or other terms). The typology classifies a victim of rare, but serious, assaults in the intermittent category while someone who reported frequent shoves and pushes will be classified as a chronic victim of domestic assault.[6]

Figures 3.6 and 3.7 (and Table A.3.6) show the proportion of BCS respondents classified as intermittent and chronic victims. Of the 23% of women who had experienced at least one incident of domestic assault in

---

6   As only details of the most recent incident were gathered, it was not possible to classify victims according to the seriousness of incidents experienced.

Figure 3.6 Proportion of 16- to 59-year-olds, victims of domestic assault in lifetime

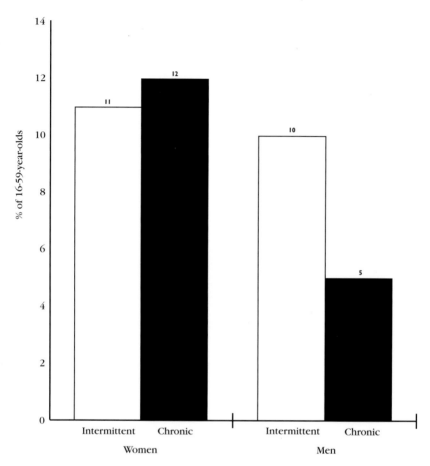

Figure 3.7 Proportion of 16- to 59-year-olds, victims of domestic assault in last year

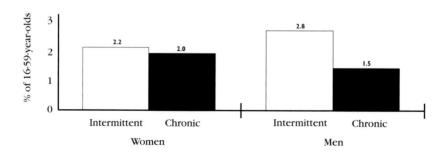

their lives, 11% were classified as intermittent, and 12% as chronic victims. For the 15% of male domestic assault victims, the figures were 10% and 5% respectively. Last-year prevalence shows a similar pattern, with the 4.2% of female victims evenly split between intermittent and chronic victims. Male victims were more often classified as intermittent (2.8%) than chronic (1.5%).

Overall then, women were far more likely to be classified as chronic victims than men. A far larger proportion of female victims of domestic assault had suffered repeated victimisation. In total, three-quarters (73%) of the chronic victims were women.

Sample sizes for victim and incident analysis

The next chapter describes the characteristics of 'last-year' victims. Victims who had not been victimised in the last year are not included because some of their characteristics at the time of the BCS interview (such as employment status) may not have applied at the time of their victimisation. The sample of last-year domestic assault victims is: 158 female chronic, 76 male chronic, 153 female intermittent, 138 male intermittent (Table A.3.7).

Chapters 5 to 7 consider details of incidents of domestic assault. To maximise the number of incidents on which findings are based, the full sample of life-time victims is used: 888 female chronic, 288 male chronic, 679 female intermittent, 501 male intermittent.

4 The victims

This chapter describes the socio-demographic profiles and lifestyles of victims of domestic assault. As the patterns for frightening threats are broadly similar to those for assault, they are not separately discussed here. They are given in Tables A.4.1 (women) and A.4.2 (men) in Appendix A.

Because information collected about respondents may not have applied at the time they were last victimised, only those experiencing domestic violence in the previous year are counted as 'victims' here. Nevertheless, some victim's circumstances, such as current separation from a partner, may be the consequence of earlier victimisation. It should also be remembered that showing that victims are more likely to have certain characteristics than non-victims, does not mean that these characteristics in themselves increase risk of victimisation. Reviews of the risk factors in partner violence have concluded that socio-economic factors such as those described here are strong but not sufficient predictors of such violence (Smith, 1989; Kaufman Kantor and Jasinski, 1997).[1] Finally, it is important to bear in mind that willingness to divulge experiences to the survey may vary for different groups of people - such as those from different social classes - and that apparently different levels of risk reflect this to some extent.

Sex

The degree to which men are victims of domestic violence is controversial. Some commentators claim that women are as violent as men in couple relationships (Lucal, 1995; Henman, 1996; Carrado et al, 1996). A more common view is that women are the main victims of domestic violence. It is argued that men commit assaults more frequently and more severely, and that women suffer greater direct and indirect consequences of such victimisation (eg Nazroo, 1995; Browne, 1993). Underpinning this view is the greater average physical strength of men and their more dominant role in sexual victimisation. Also, greater economic dependence and responsibility

---

1   Other factors not measured here that have been identified as important include: the dynamics of power and control, self-esteem, and family history.

for children are factors that tend to make it more difficult for women than men to leave violent relationships.

In the event, the CASI method found relatively high levels of male victimisation, to the extent that men appear to be at equal risk to women of domestic assault (4.2% of both sexes reported an assault in the last year). But, as discussed in Chapter 5, women's chances of serious assault are greater than men's, on average. And, as shown in Chapter 3, women are far more likely than men to be repeatedly assaulted.

Age

Chapter 3 showed the current age profile of life-time victims. Looking at the age of last-year victims on the other hand shows at what age violence is most likely to occur. The young appear to be at greatest risk: 10.1% of women aged 16 to 19 and 9.2% of those aged 20 to 24 said they had been assaulted by a partner within the last year. The peak age for men was 20 to 24: 9.2% said they had been assaulted in the previous year (Figure 4.1). Although risks of partner assault decrease with age for both men and women, they do not disappear - around 1% of the over 45s had been assaulted by a partner in the last year.

Figure 4.1 Prevalence of domestic assault in 1995, by age

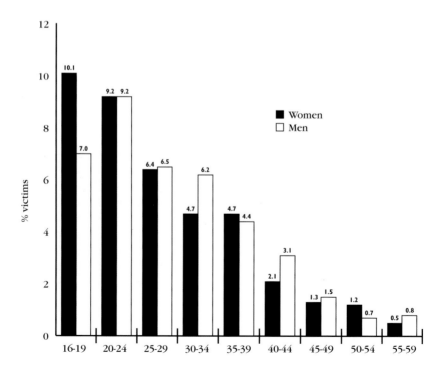

Ethnic group

Amongst women, risks of domestic violence do not differ significantly by ethnic origin: about 4% of all ethnic groups said they had been victims in 1995. The pattern was somewhat different for men. Asian men were much less likely than white men to say they had been assaulted by a partner (Figure 4.2).

Figure 4.2 Risks of domestic assault in 1995, by ethnic group

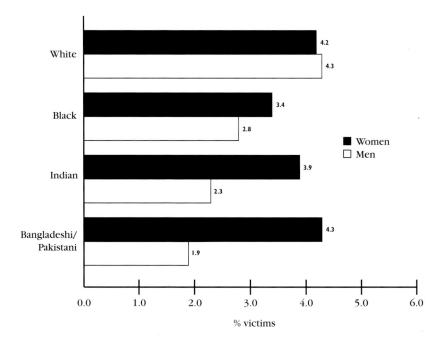

% victims

Marital status

Women who described themselves as currently separated from a partner with whom they had previously been living were by far the most likely to have been victims of domestic assault in the previous year: 22% had been assaulted at least once in 1995. While for some of this group separation may have followed the assault, the weight of evidence suggests many assaults occur immediately following separation (Edwards, 1989, Hart et al, 1990). At lowest risk are married women (2%), followed by those co-habiting (3%). Risks are higher for single women - both the never married (8%) and now divorced (6%).

Married men are also at lowest risk (3%), but at greatest risk are the non-married co-habiting (8%) rather than the separated (5%). This perhaps reflects differential emotional reactions to separation on the part of men and women, with women less likely to use violence than men to express their feelings in this context. Women's violence against men is, therefore, more likely to be within the context of an ongoing relationship.

Employment status

Women who work outside the home are at lower risk than those who are not earning. At highest risk are students (overall, 6% were assaulted in the previous year), houseworkers (6%)[2], and the unemployed. Overall levels of risk among men in these three groups were similar.

This pattern is explained in part by age: the unemployed and students tend to be younger. But the amount of time spent in the home by these groups may also be a factor: risks for older female houseworkers are higher than the average for the age group (Table 4.1). Risks for those who spend more time at home may also be heightened by other factors, such as the presence of children in the household, ill health and/or the financial stress of unemployment.

Table 4.1 Prevalence of domestic assault in 1995, by employment status

	Women		Men	
	16 to 29 %	30 to 59 %	16 to 29 %	30 to 59 %
Full-time work	5.9	1.9	7.4	2.9
Part-time work	9.6	2.0	8.9	2.1
Student	7.3	-	4.4	-
Houseworker	11.5	4.4	-	-
Unemployed	13.1	3.2	10.6	3.2
All	8.2	2.6	7.4	2.9

Note:
1. Source: 1996 BCS, CASI questionnaire.
2. '-' indicates too few cases for reliable analysis.

Social class

One measure of social class is given by a classification of occupations, ranging from 'professional' to 'unskilled'. Women living in households whose head of household's occupation fell in the two least skilled categories

---

2   Houseworker refers here to people whose main occupation is looking after the family or home.

reported the highest rates of assault in the previous year (6%). Women in 'professional' households reported lower rates (3%).

Tenure

Amongst women, those living in council or housing association owned properties were the most likely to report recent domestic assault to the survey (8% did so). Private tenants, who tend to be younger, were also at fairly high risk (6%). Home owners were at lowest risk: 3% had been assaulted in the previous year. The pattern for men was somewhat different. Private tenants reported the highest levels of assault (6%), with home owners and council/housing association tenants at equal risk (4%).

Financial status

The proportion of women assaulted by a partner in the last year was far higher in the lower income households (Figure 4.3). Risks for men were more evenly spread.

Figure 4.3 Risks of domestic assault in 1995, by household income

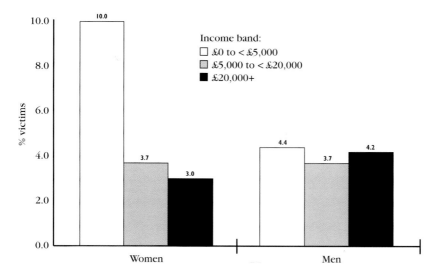

As well as measuring household income, which takes no account of households costs, the BCS assessed financial security with a question on how well people thought they were managing on their income. People living in households that were getting into financial difficulties were at far highest risk of domestic violence. 10% of women and 12% of men living in these households had been assaulted in the previous year, perhaps suggesting that financial pressures are likely to lead to the types of tension within relationships that sometimes find violent expression. Risks were also above average in those households where they were just 'getting by' financially, but had no money to save. Risks were lowest in households that were financially secure.

Children

Overall, children in the household increased risk of partner assault, perhaps suggesting children sometimes increase pressures in relationships (Table 4.2). This was particularly evident for women aged 30-59, for whom risks were over three times higher than for those without children. Among men and younger women, having children at home also increased risk, but less so than amongst older women.

Table 4.2 Prevalence of domestic assault in 1995, by whether children in household

	Women		Men	
	16 to 29	30 to 59	16 to 29	30 to 59
	%	%	%	%
No children in household	6.5	1.2	6.5	2.0
Children in household	10.4	4.3	9.6	4.2
All	8.2	2.6	7.4	2.9

Health/disability

Victimisation levels are highest amongst those describing their health as very or fairly bad. It is not possible to determine whether poor health is a precursor to victimisation, or a direct or indirect consequence of it. There was no health effect for men, but as the question on health was a self-diagnosis, it may be that men are less willing to admit to ill health.

Disability and long standing illness are also related to risks of victimisation, particularly for young men (Table 4.3). Over one in ten young men with a long standing illness or disability said they had been assaulted by a partner in the previous year. Amongst women, only limiting disabilities (ie those that the respondent said limited their activities in some way) seem to increase risk of assault, but then quite markedly so.

Table 4.3 Prevalence of domestic assault in 1995, by disability/long standing illness

	Women 16 to 29 %	30 to 59 %	Men 16 to 29 %	30 to 59 %
No long standing illness/disability	7.8	2.2	6.8	3.0
Non-limiting illness/disability	5.5	2.6	10.3	2.5
Limiting illness/disability	12.0	4.5	12.1	2.7
All	8.2	2.6	7.4	2.9

Note:
1.   Definition of 'long standing illness' is 'anything that has troubled you over a period of time or that is likely to affect you over a period of time'. A limiting disability is one which 'limits your activities in any way'.

Drinking and drug use

Victims of domestic assault have far higher levels of alcohol consumption than non-victims. Risks increase with increasing levels of drinking for both men and women victims. Again, this might either be a cause or a consequence of victimisation.

Victims were also far more likely to say they had recently used illegal drugs. A fairly small minority of the BCS sample of 16- to 59-year-olds said they had used at least one illegal drug in the last year: 13% of men and 8% of women. Of these, 11% (men) and 15% (women) said they had been assaulted by a partner within the year - much higher figures than those reported by non-drug users (3% and 3% respectively).

Region of the country

For women, risks of domestic victimisation are higher in inner city areas than elsewhere: 7% said they had been assaulted in the previous year, compared to 4% in urban and suburban areas. Risks are lowest in the rural villages, at 2%. Risks are also lowest in rural villages for men (3%), and highest in urban and suburban areas: 5% compared to 4% in inner cities.

For both men and women, East Anglia reported the highest level of domestic assault: 6% of men and 6% of women. This was followed by the northern regions (the North and Yorkshire/Humberside). Risks were also above average in the South West and West Midlands. Risks were below average in the South East and Greater London. Women in the East Midlands were at lowest risk (2%), as were men in Wales (2%).

Neighbourhood type

ACORN[3] classifies neighbourhoods according to a number of criteria, such as tenure, employment, age of households, size of households and income. Prevalence risks for women were highest in so-called 'striving' areas (7%). These are predominantly council estates and other low income areas. Risks were more evenly spread for men, though lowest in the most suburban and rural areas.

---

3   ACORN stands for A Classification of Residential Neighbourhoods, and is a product of CACI Information Services Ltd.

5 Assaults and their consequences

This chapter uses information about a victim's most recent incident of domestic assault to describe the nature of what happened and its consequences.[1] Asking victims about the most recent incident they experienced is an accepted method of gathering details of a representative sample of incidents. However, in the case of domestic violence, there is likely to be some bias. This is because, as described in Chapter 3, the most recent incident is very often one of a series. If violence escalates over time, the 'last' incident will tend to be more 'serious'. The 'last' incident may also have been unique in being the final straw for some victims. Also, it is understandable if victims reported details of their most serious, or most typical experience, rather than strictly the most recent.

Perpetrator or victim?

It is rarely a requirement of measures of violent victimisation that 'victims' did not use violence themselves, either to defend themselves, or even to precipitate the resulting attack. However, probably due to the context of a victimisation survey and the wording of questions, the majority of incidents reported to the survey were ones in which the respondent said they were attacked first.[2] Overall, victims claimed they used no force at all in 54% of incidents - and men were slightly more likely to say this than women (Table 5.1). Twelve per cent claimed they could not remember the order of events, 31% said they were attacked first and then responded, and just 4% admitted they had attacked first (although with what provocation we do not know). Women were slightly more likely to say they had attacked first than men.

---

1 Table A.5.1 shows how long ago the 'most recent' incident was. Overall, 22% were within the last year, 35% 1 to 5 years ago, 21% 6 to 10 years ago, 19% more than 10 years ago. 3% could not remember.
2 Respondents were only asked whether they had used physical violence first, not whether they had used verbal or other non-physical abuse first. There may also be cases where the 'victim' did use some minor physical force but did not perceive it as such.

Table 5.1   Involvement of victim in assault

	Female - chronic	Female - inter- mittent	Male - chronic	Male - inter- mittent	All
	%	%	%	%	%
No force used by victim	51	51	54	61	54
Assailant attacked victim first, victim responded	35	27	32	28	31
Victim attacked assailant first	2	8	2	2	4
Can't remember	11	15	12	9	12

Notes:
1.   Source 1996 BCS.

When victims did use force, they nearly always claimed it was just enough to defend themselves (Table 5.2). In only 5% of all incidents did the victim say they had used more force than was necessary for defence purposes, and there was little difference between the types of victim in this respect.[3]

Table 5.2   Degree of force used by victim

	Female - chronic	Female - inter- mittent	Male - chronic	Male - inter- mittent	All
	%	%	%	%	%
No force used by victim	51	51	54	61	54
Victim used enough force to defend self	37	30	35	33	34
Victim used more force than required to defend self	4	8	5	3	5
Can't remember	9	12	6	4	8

Notes:
1.   Source 1996 BCS.
2.   Based on all incidents in which the victim used physical force, irrespective of who initiated the incident.

Nature of violence

Pushing, shoving and grabbing were the most common types of violence - almost two-thirds of domestic assaults involved this type of action (Figure 5.1 and Table A.5.2). The assailant kicked, slapped or hit the victim with their fist in nearly half of incidents (47%). Throwing objects at the victim was also

---

3   Given that in nearly half of incidents the respondent said they used some force (so the perpetrator must also have experienced 'domestic assault'), the proportion of incidents in which the respondent said they were the perpetrator seems on the low side.

Figure 5.1 Nature of violence used in domestic assaults

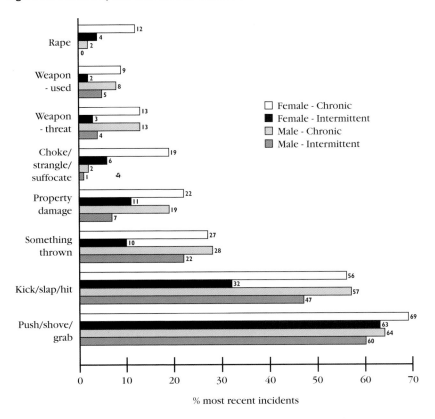

% most recent incidents

fairly common (21%). Less common were choking, strangling or suffocating - though nearly one in ten victims said they had suffered this during their last assault. Weapons were used to threaten or to attack in less than one in ten incidents. The use of weapons was, though, much more common against chronic than intermittent victims. No information was collected on the type of weapon used.

Types of violence were broadly similar for male and female victims, with two exceptions. Women were much more likely to report choking, strangling and suffocation and being forced to have sex. Of chronic female victims, 12% said they had been forced to have sex in the last incident.

Injury

The victim was injured in 41% of incidents (Table A.5.3). Women were more likely to be injured (47%) than men (31%), with chronic female victims reporting injury in 58% of last incidents. Bruising was the most common

Figure 5.2 Injury resulting from domestic assaults

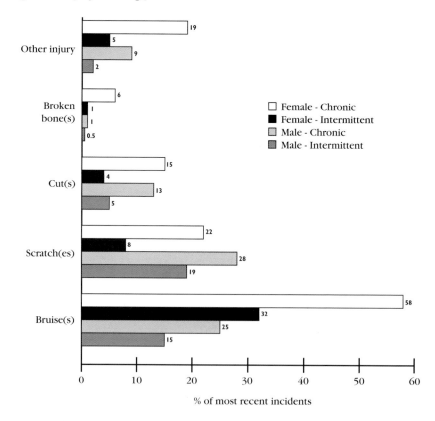

% of most recent incidents

type of injury (35% of incidents), followed by scratches (18%) and cuts (9%) (Figure 5.2). Two per cent resulted in broken bones - mainly in incidents against chronic female victims.

Female chronic victims were by far the most likely to seek medical help. A fifth had done so after their most recent incident. But this was not always due to physical injury alone: the half of women who saw a doctor or went to hospital said that it was wholly or partly for emotional or other reasons (Table A.5.4).

Emotional effects

Most of the incidents reported to the survey had upset the victim in some way. Women expressed the most emotional upset: nearly all (90%) of chronic female victims and three-quarters of intermittent female victims said they had been very upset on the last occasion (Figure 5.3 and Table A.5.5). Although women were more likely to admit having been affected, about a fifth of male victims said they had been very upset, and a further fifth fairly upset. One cannot discount, of course, the possibility that men may have been more reluctant to admit emotional distress.

Where male and female victims differed considerably was in the level of fear they experienced. Eighty per cent of chronic female victims and 52% of intermittent female victims said they had been very frightened during the incident, compared with just 11% of chronic male victims and 5% of intermittent male victims. Again, one cannot discount the possibility that men are not as ready to admit this, but it is an indication that men do not tend to feel as physically threatened by their partners as women.

The effects were also longer lasting for women than for men, with 38% of chronic female victims saying they were still upset at the time of the interview, compared to 11% of chronic male victims.

Figure 5.3 Proportion of victims upset by last incident

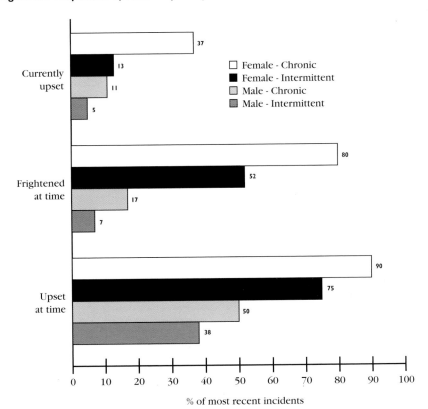

% of most recent incidents

Self-blame

Many victims of domestic assaults feel to blame in some way for what happened, either because they believe they provoked the attack physically or verbally, or feel they could have done something to prevent it happening. It was inappropriate, of course, to ask whether the victim thought the attack was in any way justifiable. But it was considered valuable to ask about self-blame, to explore whether this was an inhibiting factor in seeking outside help (see Chapter 8).

Very few victims of domestic assault thought they were totally to blame for the most recent attack (Figure 5.4). Male victims were more likely to perceive some self-blame than female victims. Least likely to blame themselves in any way were the chronic female victims, although 28% still thought they had to take some responsibility for their most recent attack.

Victims were also asked whether they thought there was anything they could have done to have prevented an incident. Although clearly the onus is on assailants not to use violence in the first place, it is interesting to know

Figure 5.4 Proportion of victims feeling to blame in some way for last assault

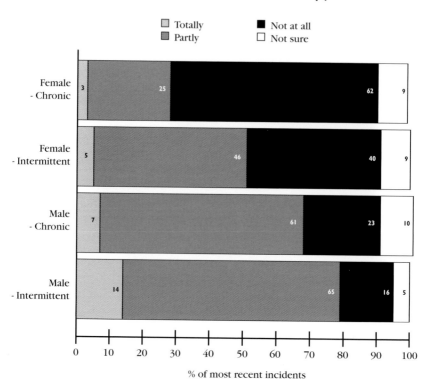

% of most recent incidents

whether victims felt they could diffuse situations. Most victims did not feel they could have prevented incidents, and again it was the female chronic victims who were most likely to say this: 75% felt there was nothing they could have done (Table 5.3). For this group, repeated experiences had perhaps shown them their lack of control or influence over the situation. These feelings are also likely to reflect the loss of self-esteem that is known to accompany repeated verbal and physical abuse (Jasinski and Williams, 1997). Of those victims who did feel they could have prevented the assault, only a minority felt they had actually tried hard to prevent it.

Table 5.3 Did victim feel they could have prevented incident?

	Female - chronic	Female - inter- mittent	Male - chronic	Male - inter- mittent	All
	%	%	%	%	%
Yes - and tried hard	5	4	7	7	5
Yes - and tried a bit	5	11	16	19	11
Yes - but did not try	2	10	6	16	8
No	75	56	47	42	58
Not sure	14	20	25	16	17

Notes:
1.   Source 1996 BCS.

Presence of children

Half of those who had suffered violence from a partner or ex-partner in the previous year were living with children aged under 16 (Table 5.4). They were asked whether the children had seen or heard what had happened during the last incident of violence. Overall, 29% said the children had been aware of what was going on. Children were much more often witnesses to violence against women who had suffered repeated violence: 45% of these women said children were aware of the last incident.[4]

---

[4]   For a reviews of the consequences of the exposure of children to partner violence see Wolak and Finkelhor (1997) and British Medical Association (1998).

Table 5.4 Presence of children

	Female - chronic	Female - inter- mittent	Male - chronic	Male - inter- mittent	All
	%	%	%	%	%
% of households with children < 16	51	47	42	46	48
% of above, in which children saw or heard last incident	45	22	17	20	29

Notes:
1.   Source 1996 BCS. 'Don't knows' and 'can't remembers' included in base.

6 The assailants

This chapter gives a few details of the characteristics of the assailants responsible for the most recent domestic assault experienced by victims.

Age and sex of assailants

Ninety nine per cent of assailants of women were men. Assuming 'last incidents' are representative of all incidents[1], over half of domestic violence assaults against women are committed by a male aged between 30 and 59 (Table 6.1). Attackers of chronic victims had a slightly older age profile than those of intermittent victims.

Men were victims of women in 95% of their most recent incidents. About half of these were committed by women aged 16 to 29, and half by women aged 30 to 59 (Table 6.1). Of the remainder, 3% were committed by men aged 16 to 29 and 2% by men aged 30 to 59. The picture was similar for both chronic and intermittent victims.

Table 6.1 Age and sex of assailants

	Female - chronic	Female - inter- mittent	Male - chronic	Male - inter- mittent	All
	%	%	%	%	%
Male assailant	99	99	6	5	64
Under 16	1	<1	<1	-	<1
16 to 29	41	49	4	3	29
30 to 59	56	49	2	2	34
60+	1	1	-	<1	<1
Female assailant	1	1	94	96	36
Under 16	<1	<1	1	-	<1
16 to 29	1	<1	48	52	19
30 to 59	<1	-	45	43	16
60+	-	-	-	<1	<1

Notes:
1.   Source 1996 BCS. Base = assailants age known by victim. Total N = 2317.
2.   '-' indicates too few cases for reliable analysis.

1   In fact they are probably biased - see Chapter 5 for a discussion.

Relationship between victim and assailant at time of incident

Just over half of life-time incidents involved a spouse or former spouse (Table 6.2).[2] A third involved non-marital current partners, and one in ten, former non-marital partners. Not surprisingly, a larger proportion - 45% - of last-year incidents involved current partners. The lower proportion of last-year incidents involving a spouse is likely to reflect the younger age profile of last-year victims and the falling proportion of people getting married.

Table 6.2 Relationship of assailant to victim

	Female - chronic	Female - inter-mittent	Male - chronic	Male - inter-mittent	All
	%	%	%	%	%
Life-time incidents:					
Spouse or ex-spouse	58	49	54	52	54
Current partner	27	34	33	38	32
Ex-partner	12	15	8	7	11
Other	2	3	5	3	3
Last-year incidents:					
Spouse or ex-spouse	40	45	41	44	43
Current partner	48	37	46	49	45
Ex-partner	11	16	10	5	10
Other	1	2	3	2	2

Notes:
1. Source 1996 BCS CASI questionnaire.
2. Due to a routing error in the CAPI programme it is not possible to distinguish between spouse and ex-spouse for respondents who had only experienced violence from a spouse or ex-spouse.
3. Relationship is the relationship at the time of the last incident.

Cohabiting at time of assault

Overall, two-thirds of life-time victims were living with their assailant at the time of the most recent assault: about 70% of male victims and chronic female victims were, and 61% of female intermittent victims (Table 6.3).

---

2   An error in the CASI programme means no findings are available on the length of relationships in which violence occurs, or, in the case of victims of ex-partners and spouses, how long after the end of the relationship.

*Table 6.3 Proportion of victims cohabiting with their most recent assailant
(a) at the time of the incident (b) at the time of the BCS interview*

	Female - chronic	Female - inter- mittent	Male - chronic	Male - inter- mittent	All
	%	%	%	%	%
Life-time victims:					
Living with at time of last assault	69	61	70	71	67
% of above, still living with at time of BCS interview	25	59	59	71	50
Last-year victims:					
Living with at time of last assault	59	53	60	68	60
% of above, still living with at time of BCS interview	56	76	96	85	77

Notes:
1. Source 1996 BCS CASI questionnaire.
2. Sample sizes: Life-time base for % living with at time of interview: 590 f/c; 393 f/I; 197 m/c; 354 m/I. Last-year base for living with at time of interview: 78; 76; 44; 100 respectively.

Current relationships

Half of life-time victims, and three-quarters (77%) of last-year victims, who were living with their assailant at the time of their most recent assault, were still doing so at the time of the BCS interview (Table 6.3). This translates to a third (36%) of *all* life-time victims and 49% of *all* last-year victims (Table A.6.1). Female chronic victims were the most likely to have moved away from violent partners. Even so, just over a third of last-year chronic female victims were still living with their assailant (35%) (Table A.6.1).

Victims who were not living with their most recent assailant were asked whether they were currently *'in a relationship'* with them at the time of the BCS interview. The term 'relationship' may have been interpreted in various ways, and does not necessarily only cover intimate relationships. Altogether, 43% of life-time victims said they were currently living with, or were in a relationship with, their most recent attacker (see Table A.6.1). This figure was somewhat higher for men than women. The pattern was similar for victims of assaults in the last year, with two-thirds still in a relationship with their assailant, usually living with them. Again, this was far more often the case for male victims than female victims.

Drug/alcohol use

A third of assaults took place while the assailant was under the influence of alcohol. It is not possible to say whether alcohol *caused* the violence, whether it *contributed* to it happening, or simply reflects a *correlational* effect (alcohol use may be higher amongst the group most likely to commit assaults). Morley and Mullender (1994) suggest "rather than a direct cause of violence, alcohol is better viewed as a means of gaining courage to carry out the act and/or as a convenient rationale to excuse it once it has occurred". While clearly alcohol pays a role in many domestic assaults, the majority take place without any such 'assistance'.

Assailants were less often said to be under the influence of drugs. They were most often a factor in chronic victimisation: 8% of female victims of chronic domestic violence said their assailant was under the influence of drugs at the time of the last assault, compared to 5% of the intermittent victims. Likewise, 3% of male chronic victims cited drugs as a factor, compared to 1% of the intermittent victims.

7 Victims' perceptions of their experiences

An important issue for those providing services to victims of domestic violence is whether potential recipients of support see themselves as such. For criminal justice interventions, this will depend crucially on whether victims believe they have suffered a 'crime'. For agencies specifically targeting 'domestic violence victims', a further issue is whether victims perceive themselves in this way.

Was it a crime?

Respondents who reported an incident of domestic assault to the BCS CASI questionnaire were asked whether they thought their most recent experience was a crime.[1] As referred to in Chapter 1, most of the incidents of domestic assault were not considered to be 'crimes' by their victims: only 17% overall. Virtually no male victims defined their experience as a crime. Female victims of chronic domestic assault were the most likely to describe their most recent experience as a crime (39%), male victims of intermittent assault the least (1%) (Figure 7.1).

A disadvantage of the CASI method is that it is not possible to ascertain whether or not the incidents reported to the survey meet the legal definition of a crime. This is partly because of limitations on the length of the questionnaire imposed by the self-completion methodology, and partly because open-ended questions cannot be used as not all respondents will have sufficient typing skills to answer them. So it may well be that not all incidents counted here justify the label of a violent offence in a legal sense.

Many 'victims' of domestic assault certainly seem to have particular difficulty accepting that assaults by partners constitute criminal behaviour. This may be in part because a 'crime' implies something which should receive

---

[1]   The question on whether victims perceive their experiences as crimes was asked in relation to sexual victimisation in the 1994 BCS. The findings of this are discussed in Percy and Mayhew, 1998.

47

Figure 7.1 Proportion of victims perceiving incident to be a crime

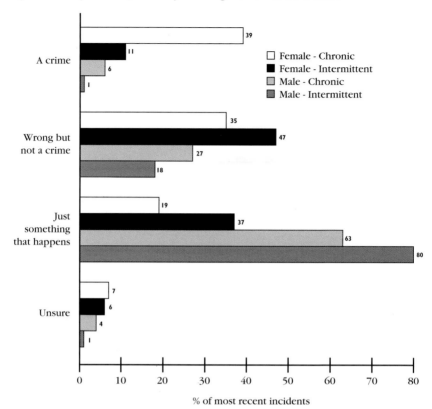

% of most recent incidents

attention from the criminal justice system and ultimately punishment. Infrequent low level force between individuals may be perceived by victims as too trivial in intent or action to warrant the attention of the criminal justice system. Also, victims of domestic violence can be reluctant to pursue cases against their partners, for whatever reason, and this reluctance may manifest itself in a failure to see relevant acts as crimes. The assessment by the victim that an incident is not a 'crime' does not, then, necessarily imply no harm was inflicted, or indeed, that no crime has been committed.

Not surprisingly, incidents regarded as crimes were more likely to be reported to the police: 34% compared to an overall reporting rate of 12%.

Was it domestic violence?

Regardless of whether they thought they had experienced a crime, all respondents who had been assaulted by a partner were asked whether their most recent experience made them a 'victim of domestic violence'. Overall,

Figure 7.2 Proportion of CASI domestic assault victims who said they had been 'victims of domestic violence' at some time

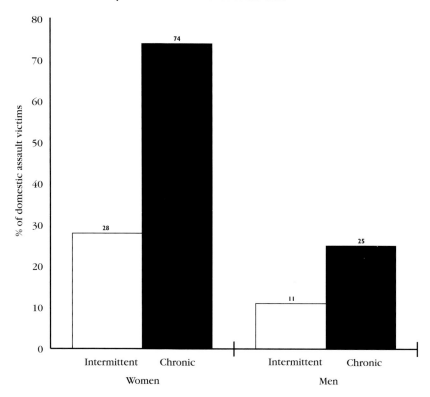

one-third of victims agreed that it had. The proportions were much higher for women and for chronic victims: two-thirds of chronic female victims and a fifth of chronic male victims agreed the last incident made them a victim of domestic violence (Table A.7.1).

As the questions only gathered details of most recent incidents, some of which may have been relatively trivial in nature, respondents were also asked whether they felt they had *ever* been a victim of domestic violence. In total, 39% of victims of domestic assault at some time said this had made them, in their own judgement, victims of domestic violence (Figure 7.2). This judgement was related to the seriousness of the incident: over half (53%) of incidents in which the victim was injured were labelled as domestic violence (Table A.7.1)

Is domestic violence a crime, and vice versa?

There is, not surprisingly, a relationship between whether an incident is viewed as a crime and/or domestic violence. Victims who said their most recent incident was a 'crime' were very likely to also say they were 'victims of domestic violence': 87% did so (Table 7.1). However, incidents described by the victims as 'domestic violence' were less often said to be 'crimes' (Table 7.2). Less than half of respondents who defined themselves as 'victims of domestic violence' said the incident was also a crime.

It is difficult to know what is behind these perceptions, but one interpretation is that some people who see themselves as victims of domestic violence, do not believe the criminal justice system has a role to play in their experience. For the minority of respondents who considered they had experienced a 'crime' but did not define their experience as one of 'domestic violence', this is probably a reflection of their own perception of what constitutes 'domestic violence'. The relationship they had with their assailant, or the nature of the assault, presumably did not match this.

Table 7.1 Proportion of victims who perceived incident as crime/not crime who defined experience as domestic violence

	It was a crime	Wrong but not crime	Just something that happens
Victim of domestic violence?	%	%	%
Yes	87	34	11
No	8	54	83
Not sure	5	12	6
All responses	100	100	100

Notes:
1.   Source 1996 BCS CASI questionnaire.
2.   Life-time victims. Perceptions of most recent incident only.

Table 7.2 Proportion of victims who perceived incident as domestic violence (or not) who said incident was a crime

	Victims who said they were:		
	Victim of domestic violence	Not a victim of domestic violence	Unsure
Incident was:	%	%	%
A crime	45	2	12
Wrong, but not a crime	34	31	49
Just something that happens	15	64	31
Not sure	6	3	8
All responses	100	100	100

Notes:
1.   Source 1996 BCS CASI questionnaire.
2.   Life-time victims. Perceptions of most recent incident only.

8 Support and advice

By its nature, domestic violence is often hidden from public view. As such, the opportunities for intervention by the criminal justice system or for support and assistance from other agencies will largely depend on victims telling others about their experiences. This chapter considers the extent to which victims of domestic assault seek help from the police and other sources, and asks how helpful was the support and advice they received.

Telling others

Over half the victims of a domestic assault said they had not told anyone about the last attack. The BCS did not ask why they had not, but there are a range of possibilities. Violence from a partner may be too embarrassing or shameful to divulge to others. Some victims may fear for their personal or children's safety if their partner found out they had told someone. Others may feel they have no one to tell and no one to help them. In some cases, victims may not have viewed what happened to them as serious enough to warrant mentioning to others.

Of particular concern, in terms of support or advice following an assault, are those who are being repeatedly victimised, the chronic victims. Not only do their experiences tend to be more serious (see Chapter 5), prevention of further assault is clearly a particular issue for this group. Although a majority of chronic female victims had told someone about the last incident (and half had told more than one person), a third had not (Table A.7.1). Men were far less likely to have told anyone: two-thirds of both intermittent and chronic victims had not.

Who do victims tell?

Friends, neighbours and relatives of the victims were by far the most likely to hear of incidents (Figure 8.2 and Table A.8.2). Of the 47% of all victims who had told someone, nearly all had told a friend or relative, even if they had also told someone else. The police were the next most likely to hear of

Figure 8.1 Proportion of victims who told someone about the last assault

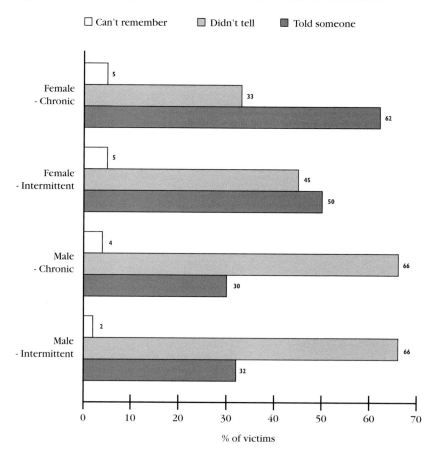

incidents, followed by medical staff. Very few male victims had informed Social Services or their Housing Department - chronic female victims were the most likely to have done so. Only women were asked if they had told a women's refuge: 3% of chronic victims and 1% of intermittent victims said they had.

Support and advice

Although very few victims talked to Victim Support, this was the group who were most likely to offer support and advice when told about an assault, and this support was invariably judged helpful by the victim (Figure 8.3 and Table A.8.3). The small proportion having contact with Victim Support may increase with the setting up, in early 1998, of a direct help line number. Increasing referrals from the police in the early nineties prompted Victim

Figure 8.2 Who victims told about the last assault

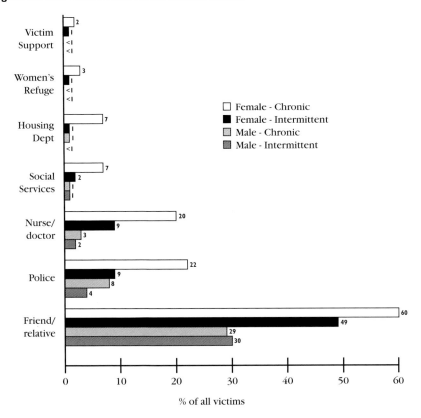

Support to establish a Working Party to review the needs of domestic violence victims (Victim Support, 1992), and to publish guidelines on dealing with victims (Victim Support, 1996). The relatively high level of satisfaction of victims found here may well reflect this proactive approach.

Next most likely to offer support when told about incidents were women's refuges, though they were slightly less often judged as helpful by the victim. Social Services also scored highly: they offered advice in eight out of ten incidents, and this was seen as helpful by two-thirds of victims.

The medical profession were more likely to offer advice and support than the police: they did so in 70% of cases, compared to 60% of those the police came to know about. Both doctors, nurses and the police were seen as more helpful by chronic female victims than intermittent. The reverse was the case for male victims: chronic male victims were particularly unhappy with the level of medical and police support. A quarter said they received helpful advice when they told a doctor or nurse, and just one in ten said they got it from the police. Intermittent male victims were also unlikely to feel they had

Figure 8.3 Helpfulness of support/advice from agencies victims contacted

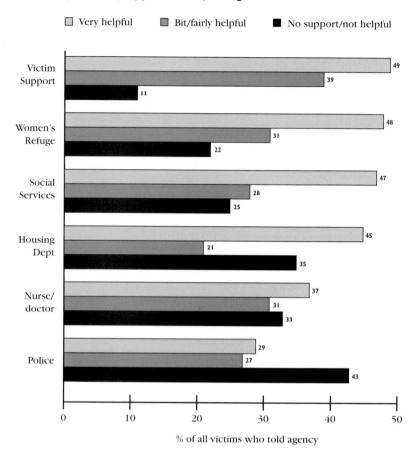

☐ Very helpful   ▨ Bit/fairly helpful   ■ No support/not helpful

Victim Support	49 / 39 / 11
Women's Refuge	48 / 31 / 22
Social Services	47 / 28 / 25
Housing Dept	45 / 21 / 35
Nurse/doctor	37 / 31 / 33
Police	29 / 27 / 43

% of all victims who told agency

received helpful advice from the police: overall male victims did not rate the police nearly as highly as female victims.

Reporting to the police

In total, the police were told about 12% of the domestic assaults picked up by the CASI survey (Table A.8.2). For last-year assaults the figure was 11% (Table A.8.4). But, given the often on-going nature of domestic violence, perhaps a more useful figure is the proportion of *victims* the police are aware of. Of people who had been victims of a domestic assault in the previous year, 17% said the police were aware of one or more incidents. This figure varied considerably by type of victim. Only 7% of chronic and intermittent male victims said the police had been alerted, compared to 16% of intermittent female victims, and 36% of chronic female victims. Clearly though, the police are not aware of the vast majority of victims of domestic assault.

The police often came to know about incidents from someone other than the victim (Table A.8.5). Two-thirds of female victims reported incidents to the police themselves. Male victims of chronic violence were nearly as likely to report incidents themselves: over half were. However, only a quarter of reported incidents against intermittent male victims were reported by the victim. Overall, the police came to know about a third of domestic assaults from someone other than the victim, possibly neighbours, other household members or - conceivably - the assailant themselves.

Which victims seek help?

Although the questionnaire could not cover all the factors that are likely to influence whether a victim tells someone else about their assault, the findings do give some pointers. The nature of the assault, characteristics of the victim, and their family circumstances are all relevant (Table A.8.6).

Characteristics of victim

Female victims are far more likely to talk about their experience (57%) than male victims (31%). Young victims of both sexes are more likely to tell someone than older ones, but older victims were more likely to report to the police and tell medical staff. Victims who were in poor financial circumstances by the time of the BCS interview were more likely to have told someone about the assault, and those in poor health, particularly so. Victims who were living with and/or married to their assailant at the time of the assault were slightly less likely to talk about their experience generally, but more likely to tell medical staff.

Nature of the assault

Victims were considerably more likely to tell someone about an assault when they had been very frightened or upset by the experience: 79% of incidents in which the victim was very frightened and 68% of those where they were very upset were told to someone else. Injury was also an important precursor to telling someone about an assault: 74% of injury assaults against women, and 52% of those against men were talked about. This pattern was even more marked for incidents reported to the police: less than 5% of non-injury incidents were reported, compared to 23% in which the victim was injured. If children were present, and either saw or overheard events, this also markedly increased the likelihood of female victims reporting the assault.

Victims who felt in some way to blame for the assault were particularly inhibited from reporting it or telling anyone else. Less than four in ten of those who felt they were totally or partly to blame told someone about the assault, compared to two-thirds of those who did not feel at all to blame. Hardly any incidents in which the victim felt they were to blame became known to the police.

Independently influential factors

Table 8.1 indicates which factors are independently related to telling others about an assault. It is based on results of a logistic regression analysis which highlights the independent effect of individual factors on the likelihood of telling someone about what happened. Thus, the more upset a victim was, the more likely they were to tell someone about the assault, but if they were also very frightened this further increased the likelihood.

Table 8.1   Factors related to victim telling someone about last incident of domestic assault

	Told someone		Police came to know		Told doctor/nurse	
	Women	*Men*	*Women*	*Men*	*Women*	*Men*
Victim very frightened	✓	✓	✓		✓	✓
Victim very upset	✓	✓		✓	✓	✓
Victim injured	✓	✓	✓	✓	✓	
Children overheard/saw assault	✓	✓	✓		✓	
Victim living with assailant	✗	✗				
Victim married to assailant	✗	✗				
Victim aged 40 or over	✗				✓	
Victim did not feel at all to blame	✓		✓	✓		✓
Victim not managing well financially			✓			
Victim does not work					✓	✓

Note:
1.   ✓ indicates a significant positive relationship between the likelihood of telling someone and the variable considered (eg whether the victim was very frightened). Logistic regression analysis takes account of the fact that variables overlap (eg being very frightened and being very upset) ; ✗, indicates a significant negative relationship. A gap shows the factor was not significantly related to telling someone.
2.   Source 1996 BCS CASI questionnaire.

There were some differences between the factors related to reporting to different agencies, when the influence of other factors was controlled for. Although victims who were living with or married to the assailant were less likely to tell someone about the assault, this was not the case in relation to reporting to the police or the medical profession. Also, younger women were generally more likely to talk about their experience, but older women were more likely to tell a doctor or nurse. Employment status was an influential factor for talking to medical staff about what had happened - the unemployed being more likely to do so - but not for reporting to the police.

9 Discussion

The new computer-assisted self-interviewing (CASI) questionnaire was included in the 1996 British Crime Survey to improve estimates of the extent of domestic violence. It was also concerned with identifying the factors associated with increased risk of such victimisation, and gathering information about the nature of incidents. This concluding chapter highlights the findings of greatest relevance in developing policy for victims of domestic violence.

How many victims are there?

As discussed in Chapter 1, the BCS is primarily concerned with a measure of domestic violence that meets the legal definition of a crime. Survey estimates, then, provide an indicator of the potential uptake of the services of the criminal justice system, can identify where services for victims are best targeted and provide some measure of the performance of the criminal justice system (CJS). But agencies other than the CJS also have an interest in data on domestic violence. Health agencies will be concerned about incidents affecting physical and psychological well being, while housing and welfare benefit providers will have a particular interest in the types of experience that cause cohabiting or financially dependent victims to leave partners. Many agencies will also be concerned with the effects of domestic violence on children.

The BCS CASI questionnaire concentrated on estimating the extent of incidents that involved physical assault, thus meeting the legal definition of common assault or wounding.[1] The prevalence of such experiences recorded by the survey was the highest so far uncovered by a nationally representative survey of adults living in England and Wales. But how reliable are these estimates? There are aspects of the survey methodology that may have depressed estimates, and those that may have increased them.

---

1   It also measured the prevalence of serious threats, such as threats to harm the respondent or their children.

Three main factors are likely to have caused an under-estimate, but on the evidence, not a substantial one:

- *The 'crime survey' context.* Including the CASI questionnaire as part of the BCS may well have led respondents to believe the questionnaire was only interested in measuring crimes, and thus caused them not to mention relevant incidents they did not perceive in this way. In fact, many incidents not viewed as crimes were reported on the CASI questionnaire: 83% of all incidents were not judged to be crimes by the victim.

- *Interviewing in respondents' homes.* Because the BCS takes place in respondents' homes, the presence of other household members may have inhibited reporting of domestic violence to the survey. Although the CASI questionnaire was designed to maximise confidentiality, there were some occasions (14% of interviews with women and 23% of those with men) where the presence of a partner during its completion could not be avoided. However, in only 2% of interviews with women and 5% of those with men did partners actually look at the questionnaire or attempt to discuss it. There is some evidence that prevalence estimates for women were depressed when partners actually took part, but as this happened in such a small proportion of interviews, it is unlikely to have had an effect on the overall estimate (Appendix D).[2]

- *Reluctance to divulge experiences.* Despite the design of the CASI questionnaire emphasising anonymity, it would be understandable if victims were reluctant to report what are very personal and often traumatic experiences to a survey. But half of all incidents reported to the survey had never been revealed to anyone else, not even a close friend.

One factor that would cause an over-estimate is if respondents exaggerate. There is no way to assess this. A second factor would be the inclusion of incidents that do not meet the legal definition of a crime.[3] Here, a limitation of the CASI method is that it is not possible to collect the same level of detail used to code incidents as crimes as on the main BCS victims forms.

---

2   This is because partners were present for only a small proportion of interviews and the prevalence rates for those respondents where a partner was present were not markedly below the average. However, it may be that partners are more likely to insist on being present in those households in which domestic violence is particularly likely to occur. If the prevalence rate for these households is actually markedly higher than the average, the overall estimate may be an under-estimate.

3   Mayhew (1994) has also suggested that measures risk 'over-inclusiveness' by including incidents that the victim would not agree made them the victim of domestic violence.

The balance of the evidence suggests that the CASI estimates are reasonably accurate, and, given the high quality and size of the sample, will give the most reliable national estimates for England and Wales. The findings suggest that domestic violence is a widespread problem. Nearly one in four women have been assaulted by a partner at some time in their lives, one in eight repeatedly so. Fifteen per cent of men have been similarly assaulted, 5% repeatedly. Risks are highest for young women (28% of 20- to 24-year-olds have been assaulted).

Levels of violence drop considerably when only looking at recent, last-year assault, but even so 9% of both young women and men were assaulted at least once in 1995, and 6% and 3% respectively, were injured by such an assault. The far higher level of recent assault for the under 25 age group is strong evidence that this is the age when people are at most risk. Even so, violence from partners can occur at any age.

Has domestic violence increased?

Although the higher level of life-time domestic violence for younger people is suggestive of increasing levels of domestic violence over time, it is probably not safe to conclude this. Rather, it seems likely that younger people are more willing than older ones to reveal incidents to the survey; to define their experiences as relevant to the survey; and, to recall incidents - which will tend to have occurred more recently - in the survey context.

Men as victims

Traditionally, women have been viewed as the main victims of domestic violence, but the CASI questionnaire uncovered relatively similar levels of recent domestic assault for both men and women within the past year.[4] Are men, then, equally victims? The findings would tend to suggest not. On average, the incidents reported to the survey by men were less serious than those reported by women. Men were less upset by their experience, considerably less frightened, less often injured, and less likely to seek medical help. It is not possible to determine from the survey why this is so. Possible explanations are:

- men were more willing within the context of a crime survey to report 'trivial' incidents that women felt inappropriate to mention;

---

4   The finding of equal risk for men in 1995, but higher risks for women in their lifetimes, either suggests risks for men have increased, or that the relatively less serious incidents men experience are more easily forgotten over time.

61

- the prevalence of assault is relatively equal but the outcomes tend to be less serious for men because of their, on average, greater physical strength;[5]

- male victims are less likely to admit, for reasons of shame, embarrassment, or machismo, the true seriousness of outcomes of assaults by women.

Whether one believes men are equally victims of domestic violence as women depends on which of the above is considered the most plausible.

An important issue not addressed here is the extent to which men and women have the option of leaving violent relationships: on balance men are more likely to have the necessary financial resources and to be less constrained by family responsibilities.

What are the risk factors?

The effectiveness of targetting prevention, intervention and support can be improved by identifying the circumstances in which domestic violence is most likely to occur. The findings here suggest a number of such indicators. Certainly domestic violence is not the prerogative of certain social classes, family circumstances, or localities. It can, and does, occur in households of all types. Nevertheless, certain groups of people do seem to be at particularly high risk at any one time. The most significant factor is age, with young people most at risk. Although the BCS cannot definitively state the causes of domestic violence, the factors identified indicate the importance of relationships under particular social or economic strain. Key indicators include:

- marital separation

- young children

- financial pressures

- drug/alcohol abuse

- disability/ill health

---

5   This will not be the case for male on male violence, but these amounted to only 5% of the incidents against males recorded by the survey.

One implication is that agencies already in contact with these groups of people, such as the medical profession, may be the most effective providers of initial support at least. This has recently been acknowledged by the British Medical Association (BMA, 1998).

Providing support to victims

A significant number of victims of domestic violence do not seek help from any official agency. One reason may be that most victims are living with their assailant, and usually continue to live with them or maintain a relationship subsequently. The agencies most commonly approached for support are the police and the medical profession, but even so, they are only told about one in eight and one in ten incidents respectively. For the minority of victims that do seek help, many do not feel sufficient support is offered and/or that it is not helpful to them. This is a particular failing for the police: the most commonly approached agency and thus the one with the greatest potential role in intervention and prevention. However, many forces now have designated domestic violence officers, who victims tend to rate more highly than the regular officers they also have contact with (Grace, 1995). Male victims of domestic violence are particularly unhappy about the level of support offered by agencies, especially by the police. It may be that support agencies have a particular problem in recognising that male victims can be just as in need of support and advice as female victims.

A particularly worrying finding is the influence of a victim's belief that they were to blame in some way for the assault on their likelihood of telling anyone else what is going on. So too is the the small proportion of victims (17%) who thought their experiences amounted to a crime. Public awareness campaigns, such as Zero Tolerance, will have a role to play here in reinforcing the message that domestic violence is a crime and no level of violence between partners is acceptable.

Appendix A - Additional tables

Table A.2.1 Number of incidents of domestic violence, in thousands, 1981 to 1995 (victim form count)

	1981	1983	1987	1991	1993	1995	% increase 1981-1995
Men	48	55	99	68	291	294	*512%*
Women	240	232	344	468	872	685	*185%*
All	290	286	442	538	1179	992	*242%*

Notes:
1. Source 1982 to 1996 BCS victim form counts.
2. Because of differing proportions of men and women in the sample to the population, the number of incidents against men and women do not add to the totals.
3. Domestic violence incidents are woundings and common assaults committed by a partner, other household member or relative against all aged 16+.

Table A.2.2 Trends in prevalence of domestic violence 1981 to 1995 (victim form count): percentage victimised once or more in the year

	1981 %	1983 %	1987 %	1991 %	1993 %	1995 %
Men	0.1	0.2	0.2	0.3	0.6	0.7
Women	0.5	0.5	0.7	0.9	1.6	1.3
All	0.3	0.3	0.4	0.6	1.1	1.0

Notes:
1. Source 1982 to 1996 BCS victim form counts.
2. Domestic violence incidents are woundings and common assaults committed by a partner, other household member or relative against all aged 16+.

Table A.2.3 Proportion of domestic violence incidents said to be crimes by the victim (CASI)

	Female - chronic %	Female - inter- mittent %	Male - chronic %	Male - inter- mittent %	All %
A crime	39	11	6	1	17
Wrong but not a crime	35	47	27	18	33
Just something that happens	19	37	63	80	45
Unsure	7	6	4	1	4

Notes:
1. Source 1996 BCS CASI questionnaire. Total N=2357.

Table A.2.4 Overlap between reporting a domestic assault on a victim form and the CASI questionnaire (1996 BCS)

	Men 16-59 %	Women 16-59 %	All 16-59 %
Proportion of self-completion (CASI) 'last-year' assault victims who had a victim form assault [3]	9	32	23
Proportion of CASI respondents with a victim form domestic assault who reported on CASI:			
- an assault in the last year [4]	73	81	80
- an assault in their lifetime	89	98	96

Notes:
1. Source 1996 BCS. Total N=10,844. Base = CASI respondents.
2. Victim form assault = incidents of common assault / wounding involving current or former partner in the 13-15 month period since 1 January 1995. CASI = incidents of physical assault by current or fomer partner (a) in last 12 months (b) ever.
3. This indicates CASI was successful in picking up far more incidents of domestic assault than the victim form count.
4. The short-fall here is probably explained by incidents falling between 1 January 1995 and the beginning of the 12 month recall period of CASI.

Table A.3.1 Prevalence of domestic violence (1996 CASI)

		Women 16-59 %	Men 16-59 %	All 16-59 %
Sworn at/insulted	Ever	49.3	56.1	52.5
Frightening threats	Ever	15.9	5.1	10.8
	Last year	3.8	1.2	2.6
Physical assault	Ever	22.7	14.9	19.0
	Last year	4.2	4.2	4.2
Threat or assault	Ever	26.0	17.3	21.9
	Last year	5.9	4.9	5.4
Assault with injury	Last year	2.2	1.1	1.6
Unweighted N		5886	4958	10844

Notes:
1. Source:1996 BCS CASI questionnaire.
2. All respondents included in base, including 'can't remember' and 'don't know': 41 on threats-ever; an additional 17 on threats-year; 52 on assault-ever; an additional 63 on assault-year; and an additional 12 on injury in last year.

Table A.3.2 **Prevalence of domestic violence by age: life-time (1996 CASI)**

	Threats	Domestic assault	Domestic assault or threats
	%	%	%
Women			
- 16 to 19	10.6	15.1	19.8
- 20 to 24	20.4	28.2	33.7
- 25 to 29	16.9	27.6	30.8
- 30 to 34	18.9	24.8	28.7
- 35 to 39	18.2	26.8	29.9
- 40 to 44	17.4	24.5	27.3
- 45 to 49	13.7	18.8	21.8
- 50 to 54	14.7	19.9	21.9
- 55 to 59	9.5	13.7	15.9
All	15.9	22.7	26.0
Men			
- 16 to 19	3.9	9.2	11.2
- 20 to 24	4.0	16.6	17.5
- 25 to 29	5.6	18.8	21.8
- 30 to 34	5.7	20.0	22.5
- 35 to 39	5.7	18.5	20.7
- 40 to 44	6.5	15.3	18.2
- 45 to 49	6.3	15.1	18.1
- 50 to 54	4.3	9.3	11.5
- 55 to 59	3.0	8.0	9.5
All	5.1	14.9	17.3

Notes:
1.	Source:1996 BCS CASI questionnaire.
2.	All respondents included in base, including 'can't remember' and 'don't know'.

Table A.3.3 Prevalence of domestic violence by age: last year (1996 CASI)

	Threats	Domestic assault	Domestic assault or threats
	%	%	%
Women			
- 16 to 19	7.3	10.1	13.6
- 20 to 24	7.2	9.2	12.0
- 25 to 29	4.7	6.4	8.4
- 30 to 34	4.9	4.7	6.9
- 35 to 39	4.1	4.7	5.9
- 40 to 44	3.0	2.1	3.9
- 45 to 49	2.1	1.3	2.5
- 50 to 54	1.5	1.2	1.7
- 55 to 59	0.8	0.5	0.9
All	3.8	4.2	5.9
Men			
- 16 to 19	1.7	7.0	7.7
- 20 to 24	1.5	9.2	9.8
- 25 to 29	1.1	6.5	7.3
- 30 to 34	1.9	6.2	7.3
- 35 to 39	1.8	4.4	5.6
- 40 to 44	1.0	3.1	3.3
- 45 to 49	1.3	1.5	2.7
- 50 to 54	0.5	0.7	0.7
- 55 to 59	0.1	0.8	0.8
All	1.2	4.2	4.9

Notes:
1. Source:1996 BCS CASI questionnaire.
2. All respondents included in base, including 'can't remember' and 'don't know'.

Table A.3.4 Prevalence of domestic violence in previous year: once/twice or more (1996 CASI)

	Women 16-59 %	Men 16-59 %	All 16-59 %
Frightening threats last year			
- once or twice	0.4	<0.5	0.2
- more often	3.5	1.2	2.4
Physical assault last year			
- once or twice	2.2	2.8	2.5
- more often	2.0	1.5	1.7
Assault with injury last year			
- once or twice	1.2	0.7	0.9
- more often	1.0	0.4	0.7

Notes:
1. Source: 1996 BCS CASI questionnaire.
2. Assumes if victim can't remember how many times, that it was more than once or twice.

Table A.3.5 Frequency of domestic assault in previous year (CASI)

	Women 16-59 %	Men 16-59 %	All 16-59 %
Once/twice	53	65	59
A few times	20	11	16
Every couple of months	7	6	6
Once a month	5	4	5
Once a fortnight	2	2	2
Once a week	3	4	3
Several times a week	5	2	4
At least once a day	1	<1	<1
Can't remember	4	7	5

Notes:
1. Source: 1996 BCS CASI questionnaire.
2. Assumes if victim can't remember how many times, that it was more than once or twice.

Table A.3.6 Typology of domestic assault (CASI)

	Women %	Men %	All %
In life-time[2]:			
No domestic assault	77.3	85.1	81.0
Chronic levels of assault	12.1	5.0	8.7
Intermittent level of assault	10.6	9.9	10.3
In last year:			
No domestic assault	95.8	95.8	95.8
Chronic levels of assault	2.0	1.5	1.7
Intermittent level of assault	2.2	2.8	2.5

Notes:
1. Source 1996 BCS CASI questionnaire. Total N=2356.
2. Levels of lifetime chronic assault may be slightly under-estimated because (due to limitations imposed by the questionnaire design) victims who had one or two incidents in the last year are classified as intermittent victims, even though they may have experienced more incidents over their lifetime.
3. Chronic assault = three or more incidents; intermittent = one or two incidents.

Table A.3.7 Unweighted sample of cases in domestic assault typology

	Women N	Men N	All N
In life-time[2]:			
Chronic levels of assault	888	288	1,176
Intermittent level of assault	679	501	1,180
All	1,567	789	2,356
In last year:			
Chronic levels of assault	158	76	234
Intermittent level of assault	153	138	291
All	311	214	525

Notes:
1.   Source 1996 BCS CASI questionnaire.
2.   Chronic assault = three or more incidents; intermittent = one or two incidents.

Table A.4.1 Proportion of women aged 16-59 victims of domestic violence in last year, by socio-demographic characteristics

	Threats %	Domestic assault %	Threats or domestic assault %
Age group			
- 16 to 24	7.3	9.6	12.7
- 25 to 29	4.7	6.4	8.4
- 30 to 39	4.5	4.7	6.4
- 40 to 49	2.5	1.7	3.1
- 50 to 59	1.2	0.8	1.3
Ethnic group			
- white	3.9	4.2	5.9
- black	3.6	3.4	5.6
- indian	2.1	3.9	4.6
- pakistani/bangladeshi	3.4	4.3	4.6
Current marital status			
- married	1.3	2.0	2.4
- cohabiting	2.6	3.4	4.7
- separated	22.6	21.6	29.3
- divorced	9.8	5.8	11.0
- never married	7.4	8.0	11.7
Household social class			
- professional	2.1	3.4	4.7
- managerial	3.3	3.6	5.0
- skilled non-manual	5.0	5.0	7.1
- skilled manual	2.5	3.5	4.7
- semi-skilled	6.0	5.8	8.5
- unskilled	7.6	5.6	8.3
Employment status			
- working full-time	3.2	3.3	7.9
- working part-time	3.1	3.5	4.9
- in education	4.9	6.4	4.7

- housework	5.2	6.2	8.5
- unemployed	5.3	5.2	7.9
Current tenure			
- owner occupier	2.7	3.1	4.2
- council/ha tenant	8.2	7.9	11.2
- private tenant	5.0	6.2	8.8
Household income			
- 0 to < £5,000	9.5	10.0	13.3
- £5,000 to < £20,000	3.7	3.7	5.4
- £20,000+	2.2	3.0	4.0
Current financial state			
- managing well, able to save	2.6	3.0	4.4
- just getting by, unable to save	4.7	5.1	7.0
- getting into difficulties	10.0	9.7	13.7
General health			
- very/fairly good	3.5	3.8	5.3
- fair	5.4	5.9	8.2
- very/fairly bad	7.0	6.9	9.5
Current alcohol consumption			
- never	3.2	3.9	5.3
- light	3.2	3.7	5.1
- moderate	6.1	5.5	8.5
- heavy	7.5	7.7	10.4
Illegal drug use in last year			
- yes (8%)	10.8	14.9	19.1
- no (92%)	3.2	3.3	4.7
Region of the country			
- North	4.5	5.2	7.5
- Yorks/Humber	5.3	5.4	7.4
- North West	2.6	3.2	4.1
- East Midlands	2.2	2.4	3.5
- West Midlands	4.9	5.4	7.0
- East Anglia	5.2	5.5	7.1
- South East	3.5	3.8	5.7
- South West	4.7	4.7	6.7
- Wales	2.7	3.6	4.9
- Greater London	3.5	3.9	5.6
Locality			
- rural village	2.1	2.1	3.2
- urban/suburban	3.7	4.1	5.7
- inner city	5.7	6.5	8.6
Neighbourhood type (ACORN)			
- affluent, suburban and rural	3.5	3.4	5.2
- affluent family	3.1	4.2	4.9
- affluent urban	4.2	5.2	7.4
- mature home-owning	2.9	3.2	4.6
- new home-owning	3.3	3.5	5.0
- council estates and low income	6.2	6.6	8.9

Notes:
1.   Source 1996 BCS CASI questionnaire.

Table A.4.2 Proportion of men aged 16-59 victims of domestic violence in last year, by socio-demographic characteristics

	Threats	Domestic assault	Threats or domestic assault
	%	%	%
Age group			
- 16 to 24	1.6	8.1	8.8
- 25 to 29	1.1	6.5	7.3
- 30 to 39	1.9	5.3	6.5
- 40 to 49	1.2	2.3	3.0
- 50 to 59	0.3	0.7	0.7
Ethnic group			
- white	1.2	4.3	5.0
- black	1.8	2.8	4.1
- indian	1.7	2.3	3.6
- pakistani/bangladeshi	1.0	1.9	2.2
Current marital status			
- married	0.9	3.2	3.7
- cohabiting	1.9	7.7	9.4
- separated	3.0	5.3	5.3
- divorced	1.6	5.3	7.6
- never married	1.4	5.0	5.8
- widowed	0.0	0.0	0.0
Employment status			
- working full-time	1.1	4.0	4.6
- working part-time	0.9	5.8	6.0
- in education	0.6	4.9	5.5
- housework	0.0	3.6	3.6
- unemployed	2.5	4.9	6.4
Household social class			
- professional	1.2	5.6	6.2
- managerial	1.1	4.1	4.5
- skilled non-manual	1.3	4.1	4.7
- skilled manual	1.3	4.4	5.2
- semi-skilled	0.9	3.3	4.1
- unskilled	2.5	2.7	4.1
Current tenure			
- owner occupier	1.0	4.1	4.6
- council/ha tenant	1.3	4.3	5.0
- private tenant	2.5	5.6	7.5
Household income			
- 0 to < £5,000	2.0	4.4	5.4
- £5,000 to < £20,000	1.2	3.7	4.4
- £20,000+	1.0	4.2	4.8
Current financial state			
- managing well, able to save	0.8	3.5	4.2
- just getting by, unable to save	1.8	4.7	5.5
- getting into difficulties	2.0	11.5	12.7
General health			
- very/fairly good	1.1	4.2	4.9
- fair	1.5	4.2	5.0
- very/fairly bad	3.5	4.1	6.2

Current alcohol consumption			
- never	1.1	2.0	2.5
- light	1.3	3.6	4.4
- moderate	0.7	4.2	4.6
- heavy	1.6	5.9	6.7
Illegal drug use in last year			
- yes (13%)	2.9	11.2	12.8
- no (87%)	1.0	3.2	3.8
Region of the country			
- North	1.0	5.6	6.2
- Yorks/Humber	1.5	5.3	5.6
- North West	0.9	5.3	5.8
- East Midlands	0.9	2.9	3.2
- West Midlands	1.5	4.1	4.9
- East Anglia	1.2	6.2	6.9
- South East	0.9	3.6	4.2
- South West	0.9	5.1	5.7
- Wales	1.7	2.1	3.6
- Greater London	2.1	3.4	4.8
Locality			
- rural village	0.5	2.8	3.1
- urban/suburban	1.2	4.5	5.2
- inner city	1.6	3.6	4.7
Neighbourhood type (ACORN)			
- affluent, suburban and rural	1.2	2.9	3.5
- affluent family	0.5	4.0	4.2
- affluent urban	1.5	3.8	5.1
- mature home-owning	1.1	4.9	5.4
- new home-owning	1.2	4.9	5.6
- council estates and low income	1.9	4.7	5.8

Notes:
1.   Source 1996 BCS CASI questionnaire.

Table A.5.1 Time ago of most recent incident of domestic assault

	Female - chronic	Female - intermittent	Male - chronic	Male - intermittent	All
	%	%	%	%	%
Within last year	17	21	29	28	22
1 to 5 years ago	31	37	33	38	35
6 to 10 years ago	24	19	22	17	21
11 to 20 years ago	18	17	7	10	14
More than 20 years ago	8	4	2	5	5
Can't remember	2	3	7	3	3

Notes:
1.   Source 1996 BCS CASI questionnaire. Total N=2356.

Table A.5.2 Type of violence used in last domestic assault

	Female - chronic %	Female - intermittent %	Male - chronic %	Male - intermittent %	All %
Pushed, shoved, grabbed	69	63	64	60	65
Kicked, slapped, hit with fist	56	32	57	47	47
Something thrown	27	10	28	22	21
Property damaged	22	11	19	7	15
Choked, strangled, suffocated	19	6	2	1	9
Threatened with weapon	13	3	13	4	8
Hit with weapon	9	2	8	5	6
Forced to have sex	12	4	2	0	5

Notes:
1.   Source 1996 BCS CASI questionnaire.
2.   Each incident could involve more than one type of violence.

Table A.5.3 Type of injury resulting from last domestic assault

	Female - chronic %	Female - intermittent %	Male - chronic %	Male - intermittent %	All %
No injury	42	65	60	73	59
Some injury:	58	35	40	27	41
Bruise(s)	58	32	25	15	35
Scratch(es)	22	8	28	19	18
Cut(s)	15	4	13	5	9
Broken bone(s)	6	1	1	<1	2
Any other injury	19	5	9	2	9
Unweighted N	880	679	285	501	2345

Notes:
1.   Source 1996 BCS CASI questionnaire.
2.   Bases exclude don't knows and these vary by item.

Table A.5.4 Proportion of victims seeking medical attention following last domestic assault

	Female - chronic %	Female - intermittent %	Male - chronic %	Male - intermittent %	All %
Saw doctor/went to hospital	20	6	5	2	9
Medical attention:					
For physical injury	10	3	4	2	5
For emotional upset	2	<1	<1	<1	1
For physical and emotional reasons	7	2	0	<1	3
For other reason	1	<1	1	0	<1

Notes:
1. Source 1996 BCS CASI questionanire.
2. 'Don't knows' and 'can't remembers' excluded. Total N = 2336.

Table A.5.5 Emotional effects of last domestic assault

	Female - chronic %	Female - intermittent %	Male - chronic %	Male - intermittent %	All %
Upset at time:					
Very	75	52	24	17	47
Fairly	15	23	26	21	20
A bit	7	18	26	33	19
Not at all	4	7	24	29	13
Frightened at time:					
Very	60	26	5	2	28
Fairly	20	26	12	5	17
A bit	12	28	19	16	19
Not at all	9	20	64	77	36
Current degree of upset/anxiety:					
Very	19	6	4	3	9
Fairly	18	7	7	2	10
A bit	26	24	16	14	21
Not at all	36	63	73	81	60

Notes:
1. Source 1996 BCS CASI questionanire.
2. 'Don't knows' and 'can't remembers' excluded. Minimum total N = 2222.

Table A.5.6 Proportion of victims feeling to blame in some way for last domestic assault

	Female - chronic %	Female - intermittent %	Male - chronic %	Male - intermittent %	All %
Totally	3	5	7	14	7
Partly	25	46	61	65	46
Not at all	62	40	23	16	39
Not sure	9	9	10	5	8

Notes:
1. Source 1996 BCS CASI questionnaire. Total N = 2356.

Table A.6.1 Proportion of victims in a relationship with their most recent assailant at the time of the BCS interview

	Female - chronic %	Female - intermittent %	Male - chronic %	Male - intermittent %	All %
Life-time victims:					
Living with currently	18	38	44	52	36
Not living with,					
but in a relationship	5	6	11	10	7
Not now in a relationship	77	56	46	38	57
Last-year victims:					
Living with currently	35	42	61	59	49
Not living with,					
but in a relationship	18	16	21	18	18
Not now in a relationship	47	42	18	23	33

Notes:
1. Source 1996 BCS CASI questionnaire.

Table A.7.1 **Proportion of victims saying they were victims of domestic violence, by typology**

	Female - chronic %	Female - intermittent %	Male - chronic %	Male - intermittent %	All %
% of most recent incidents perceived as 'domestic violence'	66	22	19	9	33
% of all domestic assault victims saying they had been a 'victim of domestic violence' at some time	74	28	25	11	39
% of injury incidents perceived as 'domestic violence'	81	37	30	15	53

Notes:
1. Source 1996 BCS CASI questionnaire.
2. Don't knows included. Base for rows 1 & 3 = 2356; for row 2 = 1062.

Table A.7.2 **Proportion of victims saying they were victims of domestic violence, by sex**

	Female victims %	Male victims %
% of most recent incidents perceived as 'domestic violence'	46	12
% of all domestic assault victims saying they had been a 'victim of domestic violence' at some time	52	16
% of injury incidents perceived as 'domestic violence'	66	22

Notes:
1. Source 1996 BCS CASI questionanire.

Table A.8.1 Proportion of life-time victims who told someone about their last domestic assault

	Female - chronic %	Female - intermittent %	Male - chronic %	Male - intermittent %	All %
All who told someone	62	50	30	32	47
% of above who told					
one agency	*50*	*73*	*74*	*89*	65
two	*27*	*18*	*19*	*6*	20
three	*12*	*6*	*5*	*3*	8
four or more	*11*	*5*	*2*	*2*	7
Didn't tell anyone	33	45	67	66	49
Can't remember	5	5	4	2	4

Notes:

    1. Source 1996 BCS CASI questionnaire. Total N=2357.

Table A.8.2 Who life-time victims told about last domestic assault

	Female - chronic %	Female - intermittent %	Male - chronic %	Male - intermittent %	All %
Victim told:					
Friend/relative	60	49	29	30	45
Police	22	9	8	4	12
Nurse/doctor	20	9	3	2	10
Victim Support	2	1	0	0	1
Women's Refuge	3	1	na	na	1
Social Services	7	2	1	1	3
Housing Department	7	1	1	0	3

Notes:

1.   Source 1996 BCS CASI questionnaire.

2.   Victim could have told more than one agency about assault. Don't knows included. Total N=2356

Table A.8.3 Proportion of victims who told agency, who were offered support/advice and who found this helpful

	Female - chronic %	Female - intermittent %	Male - chronic %	Male - intermittent %	All %
Friends/relatives/neighbours					
% offered advice/support	90	87	74	62	83
% very/fairly helpful	*72*	*64*	*52*	*43*	*63*
Doctor/nurse:					
% offered advice/support	73	62	41	84	70
% very/fairly helpful	*62*	*51*	*26*	*62*	*58*
Victim Support:					
% offered advice/support	91	92	-	-	92
% very/fairly helpful	*86*	*74*	-	-	*83*
Women's Refuge					
% offered advice/support	84	91	n.a.	n.a.	86
% very/fairly helpful	*72*	*36*	*n.a.*	*n.a.*	*63*
Social Services					
% offered advice/support	84	75	-	-	80
% very/fairly helpful	*68*	*59*	-	-	*65*
Housing Department					
% offered advice/support	71	47	-	-	67
% very/fairly helpful	*64*	*36*	-	-	*60*
Police					
% offered advice/support	68	63	21	36	60
% very/fairly helpful	*58*	*51*	*11*	*31*	*40*

Notes:
1. Source 1996 BCS CASI questionnaire.
2. Base for both '% offered advice/support' and '% very/fairly helpful' = number who told each agency. Can't remembers/don't knows excluded.
3. '-' insufficient base for estimate. 'n.a' = not asked.

Table A.8.4 Proportion of last-year victims who had at least one incident brought to police attention

	Female - chronic %	Female - intermittent %	Male - chronic %	Male - intermittent %	All %
% of last year incidents reported	23	13	3	3	11
Police aware of an incident at some time	36	16	7	7	17

Notes:
1. Source 1996 BCS CASI questionnaire.
2. Don't knows excluded. Total N = 525.

Table A.8.5 How the police came to know about most recent domestic assault

	Female - chronic %	Female - intermittent %	Male - chronic %	Male - intermittent %	All %
Police told by victim	65	67	56	25	61
Police told by someone else	31	31	29	68	34
Police heard about it in other way	4	2	15	7	5

Notes:
1.   Source 1996 BCS CASI questionnaire.
2.   Base='ever' reported incidents. Don't knows excluded. Total N = 339

Table A.8.6 Factors related to telling others, the police, and medical staff about domestic assaults

	% Told someone		% Police came to know		% Medical staff told	
Victim's sex:	Female	Male	Female	Male	Female	Male
Victim characteristics:						
At time of incident						
- aged 16-29	58	39	14	3	13	2
- aged 30-39	58	29	19	8	18	3
- aged 40-49	53	21	17	6	15	4
- aged 50-59	52	23	22	9	19	4
Not managing well						
financially now	69	25	26	5	24	6
In poor health now	80	51	34	24	24	13
Family circumstances:						
Victim currently/was						
married to assailant	55	27	17	6	18	3
Victim living with						
assailant at time	54	25	15	5	15	2
Nature of last assault:						
Victim very frightened	79	79	31	38	29	24
Victim very upset	71	50	22	18	22	8
Victim injured	74	52	27	13	25	5
Victim felt to blame	45	29	6	4	7	1
Children witnessed	81	38	32	9	27	5
Overall telling/ reporting	57	31	16	5	14	3

Notes:
1.   Source 1996 BCS CASI questionnaire.
2.   Base = all lifetime incidents of domestic assault.

Appendix B - Local surveys of domestic violence

Many surveys of domestic violence are conducted covering specific localities or groups of people. Reliable findings require a clear definition of the population to be studied, rigorous sample selection, high response rates, adequate sample sizes, and a sound questionnaire methodology. It is not always possible to judge whether these criteria have been met from published findings. Some of the most prominent recent surveys are summarised below.

Carrado et al (1996)

This was a face-to-face household survey of a quota sample of 1,978 UK adults aged 15 and over using a questionnaire derived from the Conflict Tactic Scale. Eighteen per cent of men and 13% of women said they had sustained victimisation in a relationship, and 11% of men and 5% of women, in their current relationship. The survey found higher levels of victimisation for young and single women, and higher levels for cohabiting and South living men. It is suggested the inclusion of 'slapping' as a questionnaire item may have increased the level of female on male violence. It is equally plausible that the face-to-face, household-based method depressed women's admittance of victimisation relative to men's (in line with the findings here: Appendix D).

Dominy and Radford (1996)

This research was mainly concerned with service provision to victims of domestic violence in Surrey. As part of the study, self-completion question-naires were handed out to 484 women who passed by information stands in shopping markets and malls. Thirty one per cent of these women said they had experienced 'domestic violence' from a known man at some time in their adult lives, most often a husband or male partner. A further 15% said they had experienced abuse from a known man but did not consider this to be domestic violence.

Painter and Farrington (1998)

This survey in 1989 was based on a quota sample of about 1,000 married women from twelve town centres. The women selected answered a self-completion questionnaire on domestic violence and sexual assault. Because a quota sample was used, no information on the proportion of women who refused to take part is available. The survey found that: 24% of married women and 59% of divorced/separated women had been hit at some time by a husband or ex-husband. Estimates of sexual assault are also given.

Mooney (1993)

This survey in the London Borough of Islington used rigorous sampling methods, but the 80% response rate stated is the response rate after the interview had started, rather than on the basis of the eligible sample. It found about a third of the 571 women surveyed had experienced physical violence by partners or ex-partners in their lifetimes and 12% in the previous year.

Stanko, Crisp, Hale and Lucraft (1998)

This study gives the first estimates of the cost of domestic violence, based on evidence from the London Borough of Hackney. It included a survey of 129 women visiting a GP surgery. Forty per cent reported physical abuse in their lifetimes and a half of these reported such abuse in the past year. Although the authors say the respondents were broadly representative of the adult female population of Hackney, it is plausible women attending surgery will have poorer health and are more likely to have children, both of which tend to increase the likelihood of victimisation (Chapter 5).

Appendix C - International survey estimates of domestic violence

This appendix summarises findings on the extent of domestic violence from national surveys in the USA, Canada, Australia, New Zealand and the Netherlands. Different countries have used different methodologies and definitions of domestic violence to derive estimates of prevalence (see discussion in Chapter 1). Although comparisons are made, they probably tell us less about 'real' differences across countries than about the effect of measurement choices.

United States of America

National Crime Victimization Survey

The USA National Crime Victimization Survey began in 1972. Data are collected every year from about 100,000 people aged 12 or over. Response rates average around 96%. Participants are interviewed every six months for three years. The first and last interview are conducted in person and the remainder by telephone, where possible. Respondents are asked about victimisations in the previous six months. When an incident appears to be similar to that from a previous interview, checks are made to ensure it is not a duplicate.

The design of the questionnaire is similar to that of the main crime component of the BCS: a series of screener questions are followed up by detailed questions on each incident. The survey was redesigned in the early 1990s in part to address criticisms about the survey's capacity to gather information about certain crimes, including domestic violence. Since 1994, published estimates have been from the redesigned survey (Bachman and Saltzman, 1995). The redesign resulted in an additional screener question stating 'People often don't think of incidents committed by someone they know...did you have something stolen from you or were you attacked or threatened by (a) someone at work or school (b) a neighbor or friend (c) a relative or family member (d) or any other person you've met or known?' (Bachman and Taylor, 1994). Before the redesign, the NCVS estimated 0.32% of women had experienced domestic violence in the previous year. This has risen to 0.9% following the redesign (Bachman and Saltzman, 1995).

National Survey of Marital Violence

America has seen two national surveys designed specifically to measure family violence. Using a specially designed series of questions termed the Conflict Tactics Scale, Straus and Gelles conducted a survey in 1976, and another in 1985. Although the samples were nationally representative they were fairly small (2,100 and 6,000 respectively). The response rates were 65% and 84% respectively (Straus & Gelles, 1986). In 16% of the homes surveyed in 1985, some kind of violence between spouses had occurred in the year prior to the survey. Twenty eight per cent of couples said violence had occurred at some time in their marriage (Gelles, 1997). The Conflict Tactics Scale has been criticised for its introduction to respondents as a measure of ways of 'settling differences', its requirement for victims to quantify each violent act (Johnson and Sacco, 1995) and for its use of a scale anchored by seriousness which may incline interviewees to admit to its lowest, relatively trivial, levels (Mayhew, 1994).

Canada

The Violence against Women Survey

Statistics Canada conducted The Violence against Women Survey between February and June 1993. 12,300 women aged 18 and over were interviewed by telephone about their experiences of physical and sexual violence since the age of 16, and about their perceptions of their personal safety (Statistics Canada, 1993). The response rate was 63.7%, mainly through failure to make contact with selected respondents (Johnson and Sacco, 1995).

The questions measuring 'wife assault' were derived from the Conflict Tactics Scale (Straus and Gelles, 1986) in which respondents are asked a series of questions describing violent actions their partners may have taken against them. At the lower end of the range these include being threatened with a fist, having something thrown at them, and being pushed, shoved, grabbed or slapped. Twenty five per cent of all Canadian women had experienced violence at the hands of a current or past marital partner since the age of 16, and 29% of those who had ever been married or lived in a common law relationship. Fifteen per cent of women reported violence by a current spouse.

The survey also included questions to measure the extent of controlling/ emotionally abusive behaviour such as jealous controlling of contact with other men, limiting contact with other people, name-calling and put-downs. Thirty five per cent of ever-married women reported some behaviour of these types (Johnson and Sacco, 1995).

Australia

Women's Safety Survey

The Australian Women's Safety Survey interviewed 6,300 women and had a response rate of 78% (Australian Bureau of Statistics, 1996). The survey was designed to give better estimates of violence against women than the regular Crime and Safety Survey which covers victimisation more generally, but from which domestic violence cannot be separately identified.

Violence was defined as any occurrence, attempt or threat of either physical or sexual assault. Physical assault was the use of physical force with the intent to harm or frighten. 2.6% of women aged 18 and over who were currently married or in a *de facto* (cohabiting) relationship had experienced such an incident by their partner in the year prior to the survey. Eight per cent said there had been at least one such incident during their relationship.

Twenty three per cent of women who had ever been married or in a de facto relationship had experienced violence by a partner at some time during a relationship. Forty two per cent had experienced violence in a previous relationship and 8% in a current relationship.

New Zealand

Women's Safety Survey

In addition to its National Survey of Crime Victims (NSCV), the New Zealand Government also conducted a survey designed to provide more in-depth information about the nature and extent of men's violence against their female partners. 438 women who had lived with a male partner within the previous two years were interviewed from a sample selected from respondents to the NSCV. The women were allowed to determine the method of contact (telephone or face-to-face) and time and place of interview best suited to them. All interviews were carried out in private by specially trained and briefed interviewers. The response rate to the WSS was 79%, giving an overall response rate of 57% (taking into account the NSCV rate).

About a quarter of women with current partners and almost three-quarters of those with recent partners said they had experienced at least one (of 22) act of physical or sexual abuse by their partner, most commonly 'being pushed or grabbed in a way that hurt'. One per cent of women with current partners and 8% of those with recent partners said they had been treated or admitted to hospital as a result of such violence. The survey also asked about psychological abuse: more than two-fifths of women with current partners, and the vast majority of those with recent partners said they had experienced at least one type of controlling behaviour.

The Netherlands

The first national survey on wife abuse was conducted in the Netherlands in 1986 (Römkens, 1997). A nationally representative sample of 1,016 women aged between 20 and 60 were interviewed using semi-structured questionnaires. However, the response rate was only 35%.

The overall prevalence level was 26.2% and adding in sexual victimisation without physical force increased this to 29.2%. The survey distinguished between unilateral and mutual violence. 20.8% of the sample had experienced unilateral violence, and within this group one in five had used defensive violence. Thirteen per cent of women had been injured at some time by a current or previous partner, and half of these sought medical treatment. Nine per cent were classified as experiencing 'mild and incidental violence' in that assaults were limited to slaps, hand hits and shoves and occurred no more than once or twice a year.

Comparison with BCS estimates

Comparison between the various national estimates are not really feasible. Each uses different definitions of domestic violence and base estimates on non-comparable sub-groups. For instance, the BCS estimates are restricted to 16- to 59-year-olds while both the Canadian and Australian surveys separately report rates of violence for women aged 18 or over who had ever been married or lived in a common law relationship. Also, the BCS did not separately count incidents by current and previous partners as some of the surveys do.

Table C.1 summarises the key estimates from each national survey.

Table C.1 International Comparsions

Country	Survey	Sample	Population to which estimates refer	Domestic violence estimate	Comment
USA	National Crime Victimization Survey (1992/93)	Approx 100,000 (96% response rate)	Men and women aged 12 and over	9.3 incidents/ 1,000 women; 1.4/1,000 men in last year	Intimate assault incident rate
	National Survey of Marital Violence 1985	6,000 couples (84% response rate)		16%	Previous year 'some kind of violence'
				28%	Violence at sometime in marriage
Canada	Violence against women survey (1993)	12,300 (64% response rate)	women aged 18 and over	25%	Some kind of violence from current or previous spouse
Australia	Australian Women's Safety Survey (1996)	6,300 women (78% response rate)	women 18+ who have ever been married/or in de facto relationship	2.6% (last year)	From current partner; violence = any attempt or threat of physical or sexual assault
				23% (lifetime)	By current or previous partner
New Zealand	Women's Safety Survey (1996)	438 women who had lived with a partner (57% response rate)	women who had lived with partner	About 25% (lifetime); about 10% (last year)	At least one act of physical/ sexual abuse from current partner
Netherlands	1986	1,046 women (35% response rate)	women aged 20 to 60	26.2% (lifetime)	Unilateral and mutual violence from current or previous partner

Appendix D - BCS survey design and methodological issues

The 1996 British Crime Survey (BCS) was conducted by Social and Community Planning Research (SCPR). The design of the survey was shared between the Home Office Research and Statistics Directorate and SCPR. The 1996 BCS is the sixth sweep of the survey since 1982. Further details of the 1996 survey can be found in Mirrlees-Black et al (1996) and Hales and Stratford (1997). A seventh sweep of the BCS took place in 1998, although with no CASI domestic violence component.

The core sample

The core sample is designed to give, after appropriate weighting, a representative sample of individuals aged 16 and over living in private households in England and Wales. The sample is selected via the Small Users Postcode Address File which is a listing of all postal delivery points in the country. A stratified multi-stage random probability design was used to select a sample of addresses. One adult aged 16 or over in each selected household was identified for interview using random selection procedures. No substitution of respondents was allowed.

Weighting of the sample corrects for an over-sampling in inner-city areas; for the fact that some addresses contain more than one household; and for the unequal chance of selection of adults living in households of different sizes.

In total, 16,348 core sample interviews were conducted.

The ethnic boost sample

Certain ethnic minority groups are over-sampled to include enough ethnic minority respondents for reliable analysis by ethnic group. These include people who describe themselves as Black-Caribbean, Black-African, or Black-other (together termed 'black'); and Indian, Pakistani, or Bangladeshi (together termed 'Asian').

Two methods were used to do this. The first involved identifying postal sectors with a greater than 19% of ethnic minority household heads according to the 1991 Census. Addresses were selected in these areas using similar methods to those for the core sample. The second method was focussed enumeration. This involved screening two doors to the left and right of the 'core sample' address. Interviews were conducted at any of the four adjacent households in which there was at least one ethnic minority adult living.

In total, 2,608 ethnic minority boost sample interviews were conducted within the 1996 BCS.

The questionnaire

The BCS questionnaire has been conducted using Computer-Assisted Personal Interviewing (CAPI) since 1994. With CAPI, the questionnaire is a computer program which specifies the questions, the range and structure of permissible answers, and the routing instructions. The interviewer reads questions from the computer screen and inputs responses directly into the laptop computer.

There are five parts to the BCS questionnaire. The main and victim forms are the main crime counting component. Details of the respondent and their household are collected on a demographic questionnaire. Other questions of Home Office interest are covered on one of two possible follow-up questionnaires. Finally, for the 69% respondents aged 16 to 59 only, there was the self-completion questionnaire.

Self-completion methods

For the self-completion stage, the computer is handed to the respondent and, after minimal introduction from the interviewer, they are asked to follow the instructions on the screen and input their own responses. This method was first used in the 1994 BCS and found to be very successful (Mayhew, 1995). In the 1996 BCS, the self-completion questionnaire consisted first of questions concerning knowledge and illegal use of drugs and then the section on domestic victimisation.

Respondents were asked on the computer screen to inform interviewers when they reached the end of the drug use questions. This allowed interviewers to skip the domestic victimisation section if they felt the presence of others made it unwise to proceed with these questions at that time. They could arrange to complete this section at a later date.

Response rates

Overall, the response rate for the core 1996 BCS was 83%. At 10% of eligible addresses, the selected respondent refused to be interviewed; there was no contact with the household or selected respondent at 3% of addresses; 2% of selected respondents were ill or in hospital; and at 2% of addresses the residents refused to give any information so no respondent could be selected.

Of the 5,146 men and 6,098 women aged 16 to 59 in the core BCS sample, 97% completed the self-completion questionnaire on domestic victimisation (Table D.1).

**Table D.1 Response to domestic victimisation questionnaire (1996 BCS)
Unweighted sample.**

	Men	Women	All
Eligible (aged 16-59)	5,146	6,098	11,244
Refused	118	186	304
Routed out (interviewer skipped section)	14	7	21
Repeated use of refuse key	6	4	10
Never had a partner	50	15	65
Completed questionnaire	**4,958**	**5,886**	**10,844**
Response rate[2]	97%	97%	97%

Notes:
1.   Source 1996 BCS.
2.   Response rate excludes 'never had partner' from eligible base.

Assuming the overall response rate to the 1996 BCS for 16-59-year-olds was the same as for the full 16+ sample (namely, 83%), this gives an overall response rate to the domestic victimisation self-completion of 80%.

Sampling error

There are three types of error associated with the sampling procedure: the deliberate omission of some people from the survey; the failure to interview some of those who were eligible; and the statistical error associated with drawing a sample rather than taking a census.

Deliberate omission

Some people are deliberately omitted either due to cost considerations or because they would be better covered by an alternative survey design. This includes, for instance, people living in institutions (including prisons, student hostels and women's refuges); organisational and business victims; and young children. Of particular concern is that victimisation surveys exclude the potentially most vulnerable such as the homeless and those living in institutions (Browne, 1993). However, these people form a small portion of the population, so their inclusion is unlikely to have a marked effect on prevalence estimates.

Failure to interview all those eligible for the survey

Not everyone selected to take part in a survey will do so, either because they cannot be contacted, refuse to take part, or cannot do so for some other reason such as language differences. The response rate for a survey indicates the proportion of the eligible sample that did take part. The failure to include all eligible responses does not present a problem if those that do not take part do not differ - in terms of the survey measures - from those that do. The concern is that there may be an under-representation of certain groups in the sample, and their exclusion has affected the survey estimates. Although the BCS response rate is high, the sample does under-represent some groups such as young men and Asian women. People who spend more time away from home are also less likely to be covered.

Statistical error

Because the survey estimates are based on a sample of the population, they are subject to sampling error. Sampling error is affected by the sample size, the design of the sample (clustering and stratification), and the size and variability of the estimate of interest. Table D.2 gives the error associated with key estimates from the CASI questionnaire. It applies a 95% level of confidence: that is there is a 95% chance that they actual population level falls within the range given.

Table D.2   Confidence ranges for key estimates

	Best estimate %	95% confidence range %
Women		
Life-time assault	22.7	21.4 - 24.0
Last-year assault	4.2	3.6 - 4.8
Last-year injury	2.2	1.8 - 2.6
Men		
Life-time assault	14.9	13.7 - 16.1
Last-year assault	4.2	3.5 - 4.9
Last-year injury	1.1	0.8 - 1.4

Note:
1. Source 1996 BCS. Assumes a design effect of 1.2.

Response errors

As well as the errors associated with drawing a sample, rather than a census, of the population, survey estimates are prone to various response errors. These are likely to affect all sweeps and therefore do not undermine measures of trends in crime over time. The main response errors are:

- Respondents may forget incidents they have experienced - and this will be an increasing problem with the length of the recall period and increasing amounts of crime. It is less of a problem for more serious crimes.

- When estimating calendar year rates of crime, the dating of incidents is important. Some respondents will telescope in crimes that occurred outside the relevant time period.

- Some incidents will be concealed from interviewers. This is a particular problem for more sensitive crimes such as sexual assault, and for those where respondents do not want others in the household to be aware of them.

- Also, we cannot rule out the possibility that there may occasionally be some fabrication. Some respondents may feel obliged to invent a crime and make the interview more interesting.

- Finally, there is the possibility that some questions are not understood as they were intended to be.

However, following the 1996 BCS two studies were conducted. The first was a short interview with people who refused to participate in the main BCS

(Lynn, 1997). The second involved follow-up interviews with people who had taken part in the survey (White and Lewis, 1998). The non-response survey found no evidence that people who refuse to take part have greatly differing victimisation rates than those who do. The follow-up interviews with people who had taken part showed that people take participation very seriously and attempt to be as accurate as possible.

Presence of others during self-completion

For the self-completion element, a further source of error is the presence of other people which may undermine confidentiality. Interviewers were asked to try and conduct interviews in private, but this was not always possible. Table D.3 shows the presence of others in the room at the time the self-completion was being answered by the respondent. In one-third of interviews, someone else was present in the room, most commonly a spouse or partner.

**Table D.3 Presence of others in room during self-completion (1996 BCS)
Unweighted sample**

	Men %	Women %	All %
No one else present	66	65	66
Spouse or partner	23	14	18
Other household adult	7	5	6
Household child	3	11	8
Non-household member	1	4	3
Someone unknown	<1	1	1

Notes:
1.　　Source 1996 BCS. Unweighted N = 10,844.

Although in some cases the mere presence of others in the room may have compromised the quality of the data collected, this is far more likely to have been the case if other people looked at or discussed the questions with the respondent. Although interviewers employed various techniques to avoid this, it did occur in 5% of all CASI interviews (Table D.4). Partners were actively involved in 2% of interviews with women and 5% of those with men.

Table D.4 Involvement of others in the self-completion (1996 BCS)
Unweighted sample

	Men 16-29 %	Men 30-59 %	Women 16-29 %	Women 30-59 %
No one else present	62	67	60	68
Spouse/partner present:				
- involved	3	6	2	2
- not involved	15	19	10	12
Other person present:				
- involved	2	1	2	3
- not involved	17	8	26	15

Notes:
1.   Source 1996 BCS. Unweighted N = 10,844.

Another factor that may compromise the findings of the self-completion exercise is the extent to which the respondent required assistance from the interviewer. Although interviewers were instructed to assist respondents only as a last resort, some respondents did require assistance perhaps because of eye sight or literacy problems. In some cases the respondent requested that the interviewer read out and input all their responses; in others they required help with just some of the questions. Table D.5 shows details.

Table D.5 Assistance of interviewer with self-completion (1996 BCS)
Unweighted sample

	Men %	Women %	All %
Interviewer completed	5	5	5
Respondent completed			
No help	89	87	88
Help with 1 / 2 questions	4	5	5
Help with less than half	<1	1	1
Help with more than half	<1	1	1
Help with all / nearly all	2	1	2

Notes:
1.   Source 1996 BCS. Unweighted N = 10,844.

It is difficult to know the extent to which these various factors will have influenced the finding of the self-completion questionnaire. Table D.6 shows that those who had interviewer help and/or completed the questionnaire with someone else's assistance had lower rates of domestic victimisation.

Table D.6 Prevalence of domestic victimisation by level of assistance in completing questions (1996 BCS)

	% victims of domestic assault in life-time:			
	Men 16-29	Men 30-59	Women 16-29	Women 30-59
Interviewer completed	18	11	23	18
Respondent completed				
- no help	15	15	25	21
- helped with less than half	16	22	· 36	38
- helped with more than half	11	8	18	26
All sample	15	15	25	22

Notes:
1.   Source 1996 BCS.
2.   Unweighted sample sizes: Men 16-29 = 1,306; Men 30-59 = 3,652; Women 16-29 = 1,676; Women 30-59 = 4,210.

The effect of the interviewer completing the whole questionnaire may have been to slightly depress victimisation rates for all but the younger men. However, as this was only the case for 5% of respondents, the effect on the overall estimates will be marginal. As levels of interviewer assistance increased with age, and older respondents reported lower levels of victimisation, it is not surprising that the victimisation rates in the older age group are relatively low.

For men, the involvement of a spouse or partner in the questionnaire *increased* their chance of saying they had been physically assaulted, perhaps because their partners reminded them of incidents or encouraged them to report incidents (Table D.7).

Women, on the other hand, were far *less likely* to report incidents in the small proportion of interviews in which a spouse or partner was involved. For older women, this was also the case if someone other than their partner took part. The mere presence in the room of other people has perhaps had more of an effect on the older women than the younger ones.

Table D.7 *Prevalence of domestic victimisation by presence/involvement of others in questionnaire completion (1996 BCS)*

	% victims of domestic assault in life-time:			
	Men 16-29	Men 30-59	Women 16-29	Women 30-59
No one else present	15	15	24	23
Spouse / partner present:				
- involved	45	18	21	10
- not involved	17	14	28	19
Other person present:				
- involved	11	18	29	15
- not involved	11	15	26	24
All sample	15	15	25	22

Notes:
1.   Source 1996 BCS. Unweighted N = 10,844.

Appendix E - Domestic violence self-completion questionnaire

This is a transcript of the Computer-Assisted Personnel Interviewing programme. The routing between questions (as described in the square brackets) was done automatically by the computer programme.

Evermar   [ASK THE FOLLOWING IF Marstat IS NOT EQUAL TO married, widowed, divorced, separated]
Have you ever been married?

1. Yes
2. No

DMInSHW   [ASK THE FOLLOWING IF Marstat = married, widowed, divorced, separated or Evermar = Yes]
Have you ever been sworn at or insulted by your spouse (ex-spouse)?

1. Yes
2. No
3. Can't remember

DMInsp1   [ASK THE FOLLOWING IF Marstat IS NOT EQUAL TO married, couple, widowed, divorced, separated]
Have you ever been sworn at or insulted by a partner (ex-partner) or a boyfriend/girlfriend (or ex-boyfriend/girlfriend)?

1. Yes
2. No
3. Never had a partner/boyfriend/girlfriend
4. Can't remember

DMInsp2   [ASK ......all who answer DMInSHW or Marstat = couple]
(Apart from this) Have you ever been sworn at or insulted by a partner (ex-partner) or a boyfriend/girlfriend (or ex-boyfriend/girlfriend)?

1. Yes
2. No
3. Can't remember

DMFrtHW   [ASK IF DMInsp1 IS NE TO Ever and MARSTAT IS MARRIED, WIDOWED, DIVORCED, SEPARATED OR Evermar = YES]
And has your spouse or (ex-spouse) ever said things to you that frightened you, such as threatening to harm you or someone close to you (if NChil is GT 0{such as your children})?

1. Yes
2. No
3. Can't remember

DMFrtPt   [ASK ......all who answer DMInSHW or Marstat = couple]
(Apart from this) Has a partner (ex-partner) or a boyfriend/girlfriend (or ex-boyfriend/girlfriend) ever said things to you that frightened you, such as threatening to harm you or someone close to you (if NChil is GT 0{such as your children})?

1. Yes
2. No
3. Can't remember

DMfrt12   [ASK IF DMfrtHW = Yes or DMfrtPt = Yes]
Have you been frightened in this way within the past 12 months - that is since January 1995?

1. Yes
2. No
3. Can't remember

DMfrtfq   [ASK IF DMfrt12 = Yes]
How often have you been frightened in this way over the past 12 months, since January 1995?
If you are not sure, please give your best guess.

1. Every day
2. Several times a day
3. Once a week
4. Once a fortnight
5. Once a month
6. Once every couple of months
7. Once or twice only
8. Can't remember

DMfrtTs   [ASK IF DMfrtfq NE TO Once or twice only or can't remember]
In total, then, how many times have you been frightened in this way over the past 12 months, since January 1995?
PLEASE TYPE IN YOUR BEST ANSWER
3..995

DMforHW | [ASK IF Marstat = married, widowed, divorced, separated, OR evermar = yes]
People often use some force in a relationship - grabbing, pushing, shaking, hitting, kicking, etc. Has your spouse (ex-spouse) ever used force on you for any reason?

   1. Yes
   2. No
   3. Can't remember

DMforPt | [ASK IF DMInsp2 IS NE never and Marstat = single or evermar = No]
People often use force in a relationship - has a partner (ex-partner) or a boyfriend/girlfriend (or ex-boyfriend/girlfriend) ever used force on you for any reason?

   1. Yes
   2. No
   3. Can't remember

DMflast | [ASK IF DMforHW = Yes or DMforPt = Yes]
When was the last time your spouse (ex-spouse) or a partner (or ex-partner or a boyfriend/girlfriend (or ex-boyfriend/girlfriend) used force on you?

   1. In the last 12 months - since January 1995
   2. Before January 1995, but within the past 5 years
   3. Between 6 and 10 years ago
   4. Between 11 and 20 years ago
   5. More than 20 years ago
   6. Can't remember

DMffqr | [ASK IF DMflast IS NE TO LAST 12 MONTHS]
Roughly how many times has your spouse (ex-spouse) or a partner (or ex-partner or a boyfriend/girlfriend (or ex-boyfriend/girlfriend) used force on you?

   1. Once or twice
   2. 3-10 times
   3. 11-20 times
   4. More than 20 times
   5. Can't remember

DMffq   [ASK IF DMflast = LAST 12 months]
And in the past 12 months, since January 1995, how often has your spouse (ex-spouse) or a partner (or ex-partner or a boyfriend/girlfriend (or ex-boyfriend/girlfriend) used force against you?

1. Every day
2. Several times a day
3. Once a week
4. Once a fortnight
5. Once a month
6. Once every couple of months
7. A few times
8. Once or twice only
9. Can't remember

Dmforts   [ASK IF DMffq IS NE TO FEW TIMES, ONCE OR TWICE ONLY, CAN'T REMEMBER]
In total then, how many times has your spouse (ex-spouse) or a partner (or ex-partner or a boyfriend/girlfriend (or ex-boyfriend/girlfriend) used force against you in the past 12 months, since January 1995?
PLEASE TYPE IN YOUR BEST ANSWER
3...995

Dmforij   [ASK IF Marstat = Married, widowed, divorced, separated, OR evermar = Yes]
Have you been injured, even slightly, on any occasion since January 1995 when your spouse (ex-spouse) or a partner (or ex-partner) or a boyfriend/girlfriend (or ex-boyfriend/girlfriend) used force against you?
By injuries we mean bruises, scratches, cuts etc of any kind.

1. Yes
2. No
3. Can't remember

DMfinfq   [ASK IF DMforij = Yes]
How often have you been injured in this way since January 1995?
If you are not sure, please give your best guess.

1. Every day
2. Several times a day
3. Once a week
4. Once a fortnight
5. Once a month
6. Once every couple of months
7. A few times
8. Once or twice only
9. Can't remember

Dmfints   [ASK IF DMfinfq IS NE TO FEW TIMES, ONCE OR TWICE ONLY, CAN'T REMEMBER]
In total, then, how many times have you been injured in this way since January 1995?
PLEASE TYPE IN YOUR BEST ANSWER
3...995

Dmrtint   [ASK IF DMforHW = Yes OR DMforPt = Yes]
Now we would like you to answer a few questions about the most RECENT OCCASION on which your spouse (ex-spouse) or a partner (or ex-partner or a boyfriend/girlfriend (or ex-boyfriend/girlfriend) used force against you even if the incident was not very serious.

If this happened since January 1995, you may have already told the interviewer something about it, but it would be very helpful if you could answer these additional questions.

DMpropd   On this most recent occasion was any of your property deliberately damaged?

1. Yes
2. No
3. Can't remember

DMshove   On this most recent occasion were you pushed, shoved or grabbed in any way?

1. Yes
2. No
3. Can't remember

DMkick   On this most recent occasion were you kicked, slapped, or hit with a fist?

1. Yes
2. No
3. Can't remember

DMthrow   On this most recent occasion was anything thrown at you?

1. Yes
2. No
3. Can't remember

Dmthret   On this most recent occasion were you threatened with anything (such as a stick or knife)?

1. Yes
2. No
3. Can't remember

DMchoke   On this most recent occasion were you choked, strangled or suffocated?

1. Yes
2. No
3. Can't remember

DMhit   On this most recent occasion were you hit with anything (such as a stick)?

1. Yes
2. No
3. Can't remember

DMfsex   On this most recent occasion were you forced to have sex when you didn't want to?

1. Yes
2. No
3. Can't remember

Dmalchl   Had the person who used force against you on this occasion been drinking alcohol?

1. Yes
2. No
3. Can't remember

DMdrugs   Had the person who used force against you on this occasion taken drugs?

1. Yes
2. No
3. Can't remember

Dmyoufc   On this occasion did you use force on the person who used force against you (for example, to defend yourself)?

1. Yes
2. No
3. Can't remember

DMfirst   [ASK IF DMyoufc= Yes]
Which one of these statements comes closest to describing what happened on this occasion?

1. You used force first
2. They used force first
3. Can't remember

DMdefnd   [ASK IF DMyoufc= Yes]
Which one of the following statements comes closest to describing what happened on this occasion?

1. You used just enough force to defend yourself
2. You used more force than was needed to defend yourself
3. Can't remember

DMbruis   [ASK IF DMforHW = Yes OR DMforPt = Yes]
On this most recent occasion were you bruised at all?

1. Yes
2. No
3. Can't remember

DMscrat   On this most recent occasion were you scratched at all?

1. Yes
2. No
3. Can't remember

DMcut   On this most recent occasion were you cut at all?

1. Yes
2. No
3. Can't remember

DMbones   On this most recent occasion were any of your bones broken?

1. Yes
2. No
3. Can't remember

DMinjur   On this most recent occasion were you injured in any other way?

1. Yes
2. No
3. Can't remember

DMdochs   On this most recent occasion did you see a doctor or go to hospital?

1. Yes
2. No
3. Can't remember

DMwhydc   [ASK IF DMdochs = Yes]
Did you see a doctor or go to hospital ......

1. ...because you were physically injured
2. ...because you were emotionally upset
3. ...both of the above
4. ...Or, for some other reason?

DMupset   [ASK IF DMforHW = Yes OR DMforPt = Yes]
How upset were you on the most recent occasion when your spouse (ex-spouse) or a partner (or ex-partner) or a boyfriend/girlfriend (or ex-boyfriend/girlfriend) used force against you?

1. ...very upset
2. ...fairly upset
3. ...a bit upset
4. ...or, not at all upset?
5. ...Can't remember

Dmfrght   How frightened were you on the most recent occasion when your spouse (ex-spouse) or a partner (or ex-partner) or a boyfriend/girlfriend (or ex-boyfriend/girlfriend) used force against you?

1. ...very frightened
2. ...fairly frightened
3. ...a bit frightened
4. ...or, not at all frightened?
5. ...Can't remember

DMchsee   [ASK IF NumChild GT 0]
Did any children in the household see or hear what happened on this occasion?

1. Yes
2. No
3. Don't know
4. Can't remember

DMstop   [ASK IF DMforHW = Yes OR DMforPt = Yes]
Do you think there was anything you could have done to have stopped it happening?

1. Yes
2. No
3. Not sure

Dmblame   Did you feel that you were at all to blame for what happened on this occasion?

1. Totally
2. Partly
3. Not at all
4. Not sure

DMtryst   [ASK IF DMstop = Yes]
Did you try to stop it happening?

1. Tried hard
2. Tried a bit
3. Did not try at all
4. Can't remember

DMtell   [ASK IF DMforHw = Yes OR DMforPt = Yes]
Did you tell anyone what happened?

1. Yes
2. No
3. Can't remember

DMrelat   [ASK IF DMtell=Yes]
Did you tell any friends, relatives or neighbours what happened on this occasion?

1. Yes
2. No
3. Can't remember

DMradvc   [ASK IF DMrelat = Yes]
Did they offer any advice or support?

1. Yes
2. No
3. Can't remember

DMrhelp   [ASK IF DMradvc = Yes]
How helpful was this advice or support?

1. Very helpful
2. Fairly helpful
3. Slightly helpful
4. Not at all helpful
5. Can't remember

DMnurse   [ASK IF DMforHW = Yes OR DMforPt = Yes]
Did you tell a nurse or doctor what happened on this occasion?

1. Yes
2. No
3. Can't remember

Dmnadvc   [ASK IF DMnurse = Yes]
           Did they offer any advice or support?

           1. Yes
           2. No
           3. Can't remember

DMnhelp   [ASK IF DMnadvc = Yes]
           How helpful was this advice or support?

           1. Very helpful
           2. Fairly helpful
           3. Slightly helpful
           4. Not at all helpful
           5. Can't remember

DMvicsp   [ASK IF DMforHW = Yes OR DMforPt = Yes]
           Did you tell someone from Victim Support what happened on
           this occasion?

           1. Yes
           2. No
           3. Can't remember

DMvadvc   [ASK IF DMvicsp = Yes]
           Did they offer any advice or support?

           1. Yes
           2. No
           3. Can't remember

DMvhelp   [ASK IF DMvadvc = Yes]
           How helpful was this advice?

           1. Very helpful
           2. Fairly helpful
           3. Slightly helpful
           4. Not at all helpful
           5. Can't remember

DMwrefg   [ASK IF DMforHW = Yes OR DMforPt = Yes AND SEX =
           Female]
           Did you tell anybody from a women's refuge what happened
           on this occasion?

           1. Yes
           2. No
           3. Can't remember

DMwadvc   [ASK IF DMwrefg = Yes]
Did they offer any advice or support?

1. Yes
2. No
3. Can't remember

DMwhelp   [ASK IF DMwadvc = Yes]
How helpful was this advice?

1. Very helpful
2. Fairly helpful
3. Slightly helpful
4. Not at all helpful
5. Can't remember

Dmloath   [ASK IF DMforHW = Yes OR DMforPt = Yes]
Did you tell someone from your Local Authority Social Services
what happened on this occasion?

1. Yes
2. No
3. Can't remember

DMladvc   [ASK IF DMloath = Yes]
Did they offer any advice or support?

1. Yes
2. No
3. Can't remember

DMlhelp   [ASK IF DMladvc = Yes]
How helpful was this advice?

1. Very helpful
2. Fairly helpful
3. Slightly helpful
4. Not at all helpful
5. Can't remember

DMhousg   [ASK IF DMforHW = Yes OR DMforPt = Yes]
Did you tell someone from your Local Authority Housing
Department what happened on this occasion?

1. Yes
2. No
3. Can't remember

DMhadvc   [ASK IF DMhousg = Yes]
Did they offer any advice or support?

1. Yes
2. No
3. Can't remember

DMhhelp   [ASK IF DMhadvc = Yes]
How helpful was this advice?

1. Very helpful
2. Fairly helpful
3. Slightly helpful
4. Not at all helpful
5. Can't remember

DMpolic   [ASK IF DMforHW = Yes OR DMforPt = Yes]
Did the police come to know about what happened on the most recent occasion when your spouse (ex-spouse) or a partner (or ex-partner) or a boyfriend/girlfriend (or ex-boyfriend/girlfriend) used force against you?

1. Yes
2. No
3. Can't remember

Dmphear   [ASK IF DMpolic = Yes]
How did the police come to hear about this incident?

1. You reported it to them
2. Someone else reported it to them
3. Or did they hear about it some other way
4. Can't remember

DMpadvc   [ASK IF DMpolic = Yes]
Did they offer any advice or support?

1. Yes
2. No
3. Can't remember

DMphelp   [ASK IF DMpadvc = Yes]
How helpful was this advice?

1. Very helpful
2. Fairly helpful
3. Slightly helpful
4. Not at all helpful
5. Can't remember

DMwhofs   [ASK IF DMforHW = Yes OR DMforPt = Yes]
Thinking about the most recent incident, at the time was the person who used force against you......

1. ...your spouse
2. ...your ex-spouse
3. ...or somebody you had never been married to?

DMwhofo [ASK IF DMforPt = Yes AND DMwhofs = Somebody you had ever been married to]
Thinking about the most recent incident, at that time, was the person who used force against you......

    1. ...your partner or boyfriend/girlfriend at the time
    2. ...an ex-partner or ex-boyfriend/girlfriend at the time,
    3. ...or somebody else?

DMsexf [ASK IF DMforHW = Yes OR DMforPt = Yes AND DMwhofs = Somebody you had never been married to]
Was the person who used force against you on this most recent occasion......

    1. ...male
    2. ...or female?

DMagef [ASK IF DMforHW = Yes OR DMforPt = Yes]
How old was he/she at the time of the incident?

    1. Under 16
    2. Between 16 and 29
    3. Between 30 and 59
    4. 60 or over
    5. Not sure

Dmager How old were you at the time?
0...97
Check [ASK IF DMager IS GT AGE]
Are you sure you were DMager years old?
The interviewer has recorded your current age as {AGE} .
If your previous answer is correct {DM7agr} , PRESS 1 and then the RED STICKER to continue and please ask the interviewer to amend your current age. If your previous answer {DMager} is wrong, PRESS 2 and then the RED STICKER to change it.

    1. Continue
    2. Change previous age

DMlivef Were you living with this person at the time the incident happened?

    1. Yes
    2. No
    3. Can't remember

DMnowlf Are you living with this person now?

    1. Yes
    2. No

DMlengr   [ASK IF DMwhofs=Spouse or DMwhofo=Partner]
How long had you been in a relationship with this person at the time of the incident (whether you were living with them or not)?

1. Up to one month
2. Over a month, up to 1 year
3. Over a year, up to 5 years
4. Over 5 years
5. Can't remember

DMsince   [ASK IF DMwhofs=Ex-spouse or DMwhofo=Ex-partner]
At the time of the incident, how long had it been since you had had a relationship with this person?

1. Up to one month
2. Over a month, up to 1 year
3. Over a year, up to 5 years
4. Over 5 years
5. Can't remember

DMlengb   For how long did you have a relationship with the person who used force against you on this most recent occasion?

1. Up to one month
2. Over a month, up to 1 year
3. Over a year, up to 5 years
4. Over 5 years
5. Can't remember

DMnowrl   [ASK IF DMnowlf neYes]
Do you have a relationship with this person now?

1. Yes
2. No

Dmcrime   [ASK IF DMforHW = Yes OR DMforPt = Yes]
On this most recent occasion do you think what happened was......

1. ...a crime
2. ...wrong, but not a crime
3. ...or, just something that happens?
4 Not sure

Dmvictim   Do you feel that what happened on the most recent occasion makes you a victim of domestic violence?

1. Yes
2. No
3. Not sure

DMevvic   [ASK IF DMvicitim=No or Not sure]
           Do you feel you have ever been a victim of domestic violence?

           1. Yes
           2. No
           3. Not sure

DManxus   [ASK IF DMforHW = Yes OR DMforPt = Yes]
           Thinking about how you feel NOW about what has happened
           to you, are you upset, anxious or troubled?

           1. Yes, very
           2. Yes, fairly
           3. Yes, a bit
           4. No, not at all

References

Australian Bureau of Statistics, (1996). *Women's safety - Australia 1996.* Canberra: Australian Bureau of Statistics.

Bachman, R. and Saltzman, L. (1995). *Violence against women: estimates from the redesigned survey.* Washington DC: US Department of Justice.

Bachman, R. and Taylor, B. (1994). The measurement of family violence and rape by the redesigned national crime victimisation survey. *Justice Quarterly, Vol. 11 No.3.*

British Medical Association (1998). *Domestic violence: a health care issue?* London: British Medical Association.

Browne, A. (1993). 'Violence against women by male partners: prevalence, outcomes and policy implications'. *American Psychologist, Vol. 48 No. 10 pp 1077-1087.*

Carrado, M., George, M. J., Loxam, E., Jones, L. and Templar, D. (1996). Aggression in British heterosexual relationships: a descriptive analysis. *Aggressive Behaviour, Vol. 22, pp 401-415.*

Davidoff, L. and Dowds, L. (1989). *Recent trends in crimes of violence against the person in England and Wales.* Research and Planning Unit Research Bulletin, No. 27. London: Home Office.

Dominy, N. and Radford, L. (1996). *Domestic violence in Surrey: developing an effective inter-agency response.* Surrey County Council and Roehampton Institute, London.

Dwyer, D.C. (1995). Response to the victims of domestic violence: analysis and implications of the British experience. *Crime and Delinquency, Vol. 41, No. 4 pp 527-540.*

Edwards, S. S. M. (1989). *Policing 'domestic' violence: women, the law and the state.* London: Sage.

Garner, J. and Fagan, J. (1997). 'Victims of domestic violence'. In: *Victims of Crime,* R. C Davis, A. J. Lurigio, W. G. Skogan (Ed.). London: Sage.

Gartner, R. and Macmillan, R. (1995). 'The effect of victim-offender relationship on reporting crimes of violence against women'. *Canadian Journal of Criminology, Vol. 37, No. 3. pp 393-429.*

Gelles, R. J. (1997). *Intimate violence in families.* London: Sage.

Genn, H. (1988). 'Multiple victimisation'. In: Maguire, M. and Pointings, J. (Eds.), *Victims of Crime: A New Deal?* Milton Keynes: Open University Press.

Grace, S. (1995). *Policing domestic violence in the 1990s.* Home Office Research Study No.139. London: Home Office.

Hales, J. and Stratford, N. (1997). *The 1996 British Crime Survey Technical Report.* London: SCPR.

Hart, B., Stuehling, J., Reese, M. and Stubbing, E. (1990). *Confronting domestic violence: effective police responses.* Reading, Pennsylvania: Pennsylvania Coalition Against Domestic Violence.

Henman, M. (1996). Domestic violence: do men under report? *Forensic Update 47.*

Jasinksi, J. L. and Williams, L. M. (ed.) (1997). *Partner violence: a comprehensive review of 20 years of research.* London: Sage.

Johnson, H. (1994). *'Seriousness, type and frequency of violence against wives'.* Paper at the American Society of Criminology Meeting, Miami, November 1994.

Johnson, H. and Sacco, V. F. (1995). 'Researching violence against women: Statistics Canada's national survey. *Canadian Journal of Criminology, Vol. 37, No. 3. pp 281-304.*

Kaufman Kantor, G. and Jasinski, J. L. (1997). 'Dynamics and risk factors in partner violence'. In: Jasinski and Williams (Ed.) *Partner Violence: A comprehensive review of 20 years of research.* London: Sage.

Leibrich, J., Paulin, J. and Ransom, R. (1995). *Hitting home: men speak about abuse of women partners.* Wellington, New Zealand: New Zealand Department of Justice.

Lenton, R. L. (1995). 'Power versus feminist theories of wife abuse. *Canadian Journal of Criminology, Vol. 37, No. 3. pp 305-330.*

Lucal, B. (1995). 'The problem with "battered husbands"'. *Deviant behaviour: an interdisciplinary journal. Vol. 16 pp 95- 112.*

Lynn, P. (1997). *Collecting data about non-respondents to the British Crime Survey.* Unpubished report to the Home Office. London: Social and Community Planning Research.

Mayhew, P. (1994). 'Comment on victimisation surveys'. *European Journal on Criminal Policy and Research, Vol. 2 No. 4.*

Mayhew, P. (1995). Some methodological issues in crime victimisation surveys. *Crime Victim Surveys in Australia - Conference Proceedings.* Brisbane: Criminal Justice Commission.

Mirrlees-Black, C. (1995). *Estimating the extent of domestic violence: findings from the 1992 British Crime Survey.* Research Bulletin No.37. London: Home Office Research and Statistics Directorate.

Mirrlees-Black, C., Mayhew, P. and Percy, A. (1996). *The 1996 British Crime Survey, England and Wales.* Home Office Statistical Bulletin 19/96. London: Research and Statistics Directorate.

Mooney, J. (1993). *The Hidden Figure: domestic violence in North London.* London: Islington Council.

Morley, R. and Mullender, A. (1994). *Preventing Domestic Violence to Women.* Police Research Group Crime Prevention Unit Series Paper 48. Home Office: Police Research Group.

Nazroo, J. (1995). 'Uncovering gender differences in the use of marital violence: the effect of methodology'. *Sociology, Vol. 29, No. 3.*

New Zealand Ministry of Justice (1996). *New Zealand Women's Safety Survey.* http://www.justice.govt.nz/pubs/reports/1996/victims.

Painter, K. and Farrington, D. (1998). 'Marital violence in Great Britain and its relationship to marital and non-marital rape'. *International Review of Victimology, Vol. 5.*

Percy, A. and Mayhew, P. (1997). Estimating sexual victimisation in a National Crime Survey: A new approach. *Studies on Crime and Crime Prevention, Vol. 6, No. 2.*

Römkens, R. (1997). Prevalence of wife abuse in the Netherlands: combining quantitative and qualitative methods in survey research. *Journal of Interpersonal Violence, Vol. 12 No.1.*

Smith, L. (1989). *Domestic Violence.* Home Office Research Study No. 107. London : HMSO.

Smith, M. (1994). Enhancing the quality of survey data on violence against women: a feminist approach. *Gender and Society, Vol. 8, No. 1.*

Stanko, E. A. (1988). 'Hidden violence against women'. In: M.Maguire and J. Pointing (Eds.), *Victims of Crime: a new deal.* Milton Keynes: Open University Education Enterprises.

Stanko, E. A., Crisp, D., Hale, C. and Lucraft, H. (1998). Counting the *costs: estimating the impact of domestic violence in the London Borough of Hackney.* Swindon: Crime Concern.

Statistics Canada (1993). *Violence against women survey: survey highlights 1993.* The Daily. Canada: Statistics Canada.

Straus M. A, and Gelles R. J. (1986). 'Societal change and change in family violence from 1975 to 1985 as revealed by two national surveys'. *Journal of Marriage and the Family, Vol. 48 pp 465-479.*

Straus, M. A. and Sweet, S. (1992). Verbal aggression in couples: Incidence rates and relationships to personal characteristics. *Journal of Marriage and the Family, Vol. 54, pp 346-357.*

Victim Support (1992). *Domestic violence: report of a national inter-agency working party.* London: Victim Support.

Victim Support (1996). *Supporting victims of domestic violence.* London: Victim Support.

Watson, L. (1996). *Victims of violent crime recorded by the police, England and Wales, 1990-1994.* Home Office Statistical Findings Issue 1/96. London: Home Office.

White, C. and Lewis J. (1998). *Following up the British Crime Survey 1996 - a qualitative study. SCPR report.* London: Social and Community Planning Research.

Wolak, J. and Finkelhor, D. (1997). 'Children exposed to partner violence'. In Jasinski and Williams (Ed.) *Partner Violence: A comprehensive review of 20 years of research.* London: Sage.

Yarwood, D. J. (1997). *Domestic violence statistics 1995/96 England and Wales.* Ascot: Dewar Research.

Publications

List of research publications

The most recent research reports published are listed below. A **full** list of publications is available on request from the Research, Development and Statistics Directorate, Information and Publications Group.

Home Office Research Studies (HORS)

181. **Coroner service survey.** Roger Tarling. 1998.

182. **The prevention of plastic and cheque fraud revisited.** Michael Levi and Jim Handley. 1998.

183. **Drugs and crime: the results of research on drug testing and interviewing arrestees.** Trevor Bennett. 1998.

184. **Remand decisions and offending on bail: evaluation of the Bail Process Project.** Patricia M Morgan and Paul F Henderson. 1998.

185. **Entry into the criminal justice system: a survey of police arrests and their outcomes.** Coretta Phillips and David Brown with the assistance of Zoë James and Paul Goodrich. 1998

186. **The restricted hospital order: from court to the community.** Robert Street. 1998

187. **Reducing Offending: An assessment of research evidence on ways of dealing with offending behaviour.** Edited by Peter Goldblatt and Chris Lewis. 1998.

188. **Lay visiting to police stations.** Mollie Weatheritt and Carole Vieira. 1998

189. **Mandatory drug testing in prisons: The relationship between MDT and the level and nature of drug misuse.** Kimmett Edgar and Ian O'Donnell. 1998

190. **Trespass and protest: policing under the Criminal Justice and Public Order Act 1994.** Tom Bucke and Zoë James. 1998.

Research Findings

57. **The 1996 International Crime Victimisation Survey.** Pat Mayhew and Phillip White. 1997.

58. **The sentencing of women: a section 95 publication.** Carol Hedderman and Lizanne Dowds. 1997.

59. **Ethnicity and contacts with the police: latest findings from the British Crime Survey.** Tom Bucke. 1997.

60. **Policing and the public: findings from the 1996 British Crime Survey.** Catriona Mirrlees-Black and Tracy Budd. 1997.

61. **Changing offenders' attitudes and behaviour: what works?** Julie Vennard, Carol Hedderman and Darren Sugg. 1997.

62. **Suspects in police custody and the revised PACE codes of practice.** Tom Bucke and David Brown. 1997.

63. **Neighbourhood watch co-ordinators.** Elizabeth Turner and Banos Alexandrou. 1997.

64. **Attitudes to punishment: findings from the 1996 British Crime Survey.** Michael Hough and Julian Roberts. 1998.

65. **The effects of video violence on young offenders.** Kevin Browne and Amanda Pennell. 1998.

66. **Electronic monitoring of curfew orders: the second year of the trials.** Ed Mortimer and Chris May. 1998.

67. **Public perceptions of drug-related crime in 1997.** Nigel Charles. 1998.

68. **Witness care in magistrates' courts and the youth court.** Joyce Plotnikoff and Richard Woolfson. 1998.

69. **Handling stolen goods and theft: a market reduction approach.** Mike Sutton. 1998.

70. **Drug testing arrestees.** Trevor Bennett. 1998.

71. **Prevention of plastic card fraud.** Michael Levi and Jim Handley. 1998.

72. **Offending on bail and police use of conditional bail.** David Brown. 1998.

73. **Voluntary after-care.** Mike Maguire, Peter Raynor, Maurice Vanstone and Jocelyn Kynch. 1998.

74. **Fast-tracking of persistent young offenders.** John Graham. 1998.

75. **Mandatory drug testing in prisons – an evaluation.** Kimmett Edgar and Ian O'Donnell. 1998.

76. **The prison population in 1997: a statistical review.** Philip White. 1998.

77. **Rural areas and crime: findings from the British Crime Survey.** Catriona Mirrlees-Black. 1998.

78. **A review of classification systems for sex offenders.** Dawn Fisher and George Mair. 1998.

79. **An evaluation of the prison sex offender treatment programme.** Anthony Beech et al. 1998.

80. **Age limits for babies in prison: some lessons from abroad.** Diane Caddle. 1998.

81. **Motor projects in England & Wales: an evaluation.** Darren Sugg. 1998

82. **HIV/Aids risk behaviour among adult male prisoners.** John Strange et al. 1998.

83. **Concern about crime: findings from the 1998 British Crime Survey.** Catriona Mirrlees-Black and Jonathan Allen. 1998.

Occasional Papers

Evaluation of a Home Office initiative to help offenders into employment. Ken Roberts, Alana Barton, Julian Buchanan and Barry Goldson. 1997.

The impact of the national lottery on the horse-race betting levy. Simon Field and James Dunmore. 1997.

The cost of fires. A review of the information available. Donald Roy. 1997.

Monitoring and evaluation of WOLDS remand prison and comparisons with public-sector prisons, in particular HMP Woodhill. A Keith Bottomley, Adrian James, Emma Clare and Alison Liebling. 1997.

Requests for Publications

Home Office Research Studies, Research Findings and *Occasional Papers* can be requested from:

Research, Development and Statistics Directorate
Information and Publications Group
Room 201, Home Office
50 Queen Anne's Gate
London SW1H 9AT
Telephone: 0171-273 2084
Fascimile: 0171-222 0211
Internet: http://www.homeoffice.gov.uk/rds/index.htm
E-mail: rds.ho@gtnet.gov.uk